The Mystery of God and Suffering

The Mystery of God and Suffering

Lament, Trust, and Awe

Kenneth R. Overberg, SJ

Fortress Press
Minneapolis

THE MYSTERY OF GOD AND SUFFERING
Lament, Trust, and Awe

Print ISBN: 978-1-5064-4004-0
eBook ISBN: 978-1-5064-4005-7

This title is a revised and updated version of *Into the Abyss of Suffering*
(St. Anthony Messenger Press, 2003).

Cover image: Sieboldianus/iStockphoto
Cover design: Lauren Williamson

In loving and respectful memory of
Mom and Dad,
Aloysius Gonzaga, SJ,
Robert Bellarmine, SJ,
and John de Brebeuf, SJ

Contents

Introduction: In the Spirit of Job

The woman had spent many months in the RCIA (Rite of Christian Initiation of Adults) process. Newly committed to the Roman Catholic faith, she still struggled with a profound question. Then, at an evening meeting, the question burst forth from the center of her heart. "Why did Jesus have to die?" My response was very simple: "Because he was human." I sensed, however, that her search was really about how Jesus died and how God could desire or demand this horrible death as atonement. So our conversation turned to the Christian tradition's various interpretations of the death of Jesus and the related images of God.

We also ask "Why?" about the pain and darkness in our own lives. Suffering frequently confronts us, sometimes in overwhelming ways, and raises profound questions. Since September 11, 2001, a terrible image burns in our memory: planes burying themselves into the World Trade Center and erupting in great fireballs. Shock and horror led to grief and lament, heroism and vengeance—and to questions about God. How can we hold together a good and gracious God with the harsh reality of suffering? What can be said about the meaning of suffering, especially innocent suffering?

Humans have long searched for some satisfying insights into these and similar questions. A whole book of the Bible, Job, is dedicated to this topic. At times, the search has turned very philosophical, appearing to many people to be lost in fine abstractions. At other times, the responses seem to drip with sentimental pieties but not express very good theology.

In itself, Jesus's suffering raises difficult questions (as for the woman just mentioned). In order to reflect upon and suggest interpretations of human suffering, people have also turned to Jesus's own suffering and horrible death.

Some of these approaches to the mystery of suffering, though deeply embedded in the Jewish and Christian Scriptures and traditions, fail to satisfy contemporary hearts and minds. This little book, in the spirit of Job questioning the dominant theological worldview, will address the mystery of divine and human suffering by building on other themes in the Scriptures, themes developed through the Christian tradition and yet generally held as a "minority report," if known at all.

The Mystery of God and Suffering, then, speaks to two audiences. It offers an alternative vision for all those people who, like the woman in the RCIA meeting, find themselves uneasy or even oppressed by the emphasis on a vindictive God who demands atonement. Some of these people may not have articulated this unease yet, but they will be assisted here in naming and understanding it. They will also find new light and life in the perspective developed in this book.

The Mystery of God and Suffering also speaks to an undoubtedly larger audience: all those who suffer and search for meaning and ways of dealing with this suffering. From global events such as terrorism and starvation to intimate struggles with abuse or illness, suffering confronts us all.

Accordingly, this book begins by describing the context of

human suffering and some of the responses that have been developed. Here and throughout the text we will read directly the words of Scripture and of searchers for wisdom. In chapter 2, our attention turns to the life and vision of Jesus, with special focus on his relationship with God. We next consider Jesus's death and early Christianity's use of scriptural traditions to interpret this death. Later developments in the tradition are also briefly noted. Chapter 4 highlights the alternate perspective on the purpose of the incarnation and so on the meaning of suffering. We will look carefully at this "minority report's" roots in Scripture and tradition. In this light, we can finally return to our own suffering, suggesting appropriate guidance for our journey into the abyss of mystery: the mystery of suffering and the mystery of God.

1

The Dark Abyss of Suffering

Humanity still experiences Good Friday. Mental and physical illness, poverty and starvation, wars and systemic violence of all kinds overwhelm individuals, communities, and entire nations. Each of us has a personal story of suffering. At times we cry out to God with the psalmist: "You have plunged me into the bottom of the pit, into the dark abyss" (Ps 88:7 NAB). We search for comfort, light, and meaning.

Personal and Systemic Sources

Many different paths lead to the same mystery of suffering. Personal stories reflect the uniqueness of each individual yet contain many similar elements. We experience suffering in broken relationships and alienated families, in accidents and disease, in failed dreams and boring jobs, in dying and death.

Many personal stories also include addictions, abuse, and other forms of violence.

Most of us really do not need help in recalling the suffering in our own lives and in those of family and friends. Here, however, are a few examples; the details vary in people's lives, but the harsh reality of suffering remains. (1) Spouses gradually grow apart, their careers and many responsibilities and activities leading them in opposite directions. The marriage seems dead, so they divorce. (2) The physician had been hoping that the condition was caused by a brain tumor but now concludes that it is ALS (Lou Gehrig's disease), with no known cause, no known cure. Death usually occurs within two to five years. (3) The family is enjoying their vacation when suddenly, a car crosses the median and crashes into their van, killing the mother and causing permanent damage to the daughter. (4) The teenager has long struggled in school but receives little help and no support at home. He drops out of school, facing a very troubled future. (5) Corporate mergers and resulting layoffs cost the middle-aged man his job. Unable to find a satisfying replacement, he loses self-esteem and turns to alcohol.

Suffering comes from systemic sources as well, destroying some individuals and numbing others: racism and sexism, economic policies and structures, consumerism and militarism. Depending on one's race, class, and gender, some of these sufferings may be utterly apparent or quite hidden. (1) Many people of color in the United States experience the profound effects of long-term poverty and racism, which influence individual spirits and family dynamics and shape social practices like hiring, schooling, and community-police relations. Others, with different life experiences, may find it difficult to understand or even acknowledge these realities. (2) Students who spend a service-learning semester in a Global South country come home with a much wider vision. They had never encountered such intense poverty and at the same time are surprised that these poor people expressed amazing warmth and joy. The students also experience how US military aid has helped some of these countries oppress their own people, and they see first-hand one meaning of globalization for the Global South: wealth for the few, sweatshops for the many. (3) The depths of suffering in other parts of the Global South, perhaps especially Africa, remain mostly unknown (except for a passing comment in the news) to most of us. Colloquially speaking, we just don't have a clue.

The Bible

One of the many sources we turn to in order to try to understand suffering is the Bible. Both testaments wrestle with the great question of suffering, especially in light of the belief in a good and gracious God. The Hebrews' story is a long history of oppression and pain, from Egypt to Babylon to occupation by the Romans. So the inspired writers cry out in lament and search for understanding.

The Psalms offer many examples. We have already heard the psalmist speak of the "dark abyss." Here are some other selections.

> Yet you have rejected us and abased us,
> and have not gone out with our armies. . . .
>
> You have made us the taunt of our neighbors,
> the derision and scorn of those around us. . . .
>
> All day long my disgrace is before me,
> and shame has covered my face . . . .
>
> Why do you sleep, O Lord?

Awake, do not cast us off forever!
Why do you hide your face?
Why do you forget our affliction and oppression? . . .

Rise up, come to our help.
Redeem us for the sake of your steadfast love. (Ps 44:9, 13, 15, 23–24, 26)

Will the Lord spurn forever, and never again be favorable?
Has his steadfast love ceased forever?
Are his promises at an end for all time?
Has God forgotten to be gracious? (Ps 77:7–9)

For the enemy has pursued me,
crushing my life to the ground,
making me sit in darkness like those long dead.
Therefore, my spirit faints within me;
my heart within is appalled.
I remember the days of old,
I think about all your deeds,
I meditate on the works of your hands.
I stretch out my hands to you;
my soul thirsts for you like a parched land. (Ps 143:3–6)

Isaiah presents a haunting image in the songs of the suffering servant.

The Lord God has opened my ear,
and I was not rebellious,
I did not turn backward.
I gave my back to those who struck me,
and my cheeks to those who pulled out the beard;
I did not hide my face from insult and spitting. (Isa 50:5, 6)

He had no form or majesty that we should look at him,
nothing in his appearance that we should desire him.
He was despised and rejected by others;
a man of suffering and acquainted with infirmity;
and as one from whom others hide their faces
he was despised, and we held him of no account.
Surely he has borne our infirmities
and carried our diseases;

yet we accounted him stricken,
struck down by God, and afflicted.
But he was wounded for our transgressions,
crushed for our iniquities;
upon him was the punishment that made us whole,
and by his bruises we are healed. (Isa 53:2b–5)

For Christians, it is especially important to recall that these lines were written more than five hundred years before Jesus.

Job, of course, offers us probably the most famous reflections on suffering. After hearing the long list of Job's troubles, his three friends come to comfort him. At first, appropriately, they simply sit with him, lamenting and mourning in silence. Then they begin to speak, offering Job the traditional religious interpretation that his sufferings indicate that he must have sinned, so they call him to repentance.

If you direct your heart rightly,
you will stretch out your hands toward him [God].
If iniquity is in your hand, put it far away,
and do not let wickedness reside in your tents.
Surely then you will lift up your face without blemish;
you will be secure, and will not fear.
You will forget your misery. (Job 11:13–16)

Job later objects, affirming his innocence.

But he [God] knows the way that I take;
when he has tested me, I shall come out like gold.
My foot has held fast to his steps;
I have kept his way and have not turned aside.
I have not departed from the commandment of his lips. (Job 23:10–12)

Job even wants to bring God to trial. "I would lay my case before him, and fill my mouth with arguments . . . and I should be acquitted forever by my judge" (Job 23:4–7). Finally God responds out of the whirlwind: "I will question you, and you shall declare to me" (Job 38:3). It is too much for Job, who is overwhelmed. "I know that you can do all things, and that no purpose of yours can be thwarted. . . . Therefore, I have uttered what I did not understand, things too wonderful for me, which I did not know" (Job 42:2–3). Job stands before God (and suffering) in silent awe.

An important aspect of New Testament thought is the interpretation of Jesus's execution as a criminal. This example of innocent suffering evidently called for some kind of explanation.

Scripture scholars point out that Jesus's followers borrowed themes from their Jewish tradition. These themes develop related ideas: sacrifice, expiation, the noble death of the martyr, the vindication of the suffering righteous one (to be developed in more detail in chap. 3). The hymn in Philippians offers a good example:

> Let the same mind be in you that was in Christ Jesus, who though he was in the form of God, did not regard equality with God as something to be exploited, but emptied himself, taking the form of a slave, being born in human likeness. And being found in human form, he humbled himself and became obedient to the point of death—even death on a cross. Therefore God also highly exalted him and gave him the name that is above every name, so that at the name of Jesus every knee should bend, in heaven and on earth and under the earth, and every tongue should confess that Jesus Christ is Lord, to the glory of God the Father. (Phil 2:5–11)

In his article "Can We Let Jesus Die?" Arthur Dewey writes:

> As some of Jesus's followers reflected on the events of the past, they asked themselves why these things had to happen. They became convinced that God had foreordained the events. They began looking for prophecies that would help them understand

the social disgrace of the death of Jesus. The use of scriptural citations [especially from the Psalms and Prophets] became a shorthand way of dealing with the meaning of Jesus's death.[1]

We find clues of this perspective in the following biblical passages.

> For I handed on to you as of first importance what I in turn had received: that Christ died for our sins in accordance with the scriptures, and that he was buried, and that he was raised on the third day in accordance with the scriptures. (1 Cor 15:3–4)

> Day after day I was with you in the temple teaching, and you did not arrest me. But let the scriptures be fulfilled. (Mark 14:49)

> "Was it not necessary that the Messiah should suffer these things and then enter into his glory?" Then beginning with Moses and all the prophets, he interpreted to them the things about himself in all the scriptures. (Luke 24:26–27)

Liturgy and Piety

Not surprisingly, given these scriptural roots, liturgical practices and popular piety frequently raise and address the question of suffering. Every Eucharist is a celebration of the death and resurrection of Jesus. Good Friday, of course, especially draws our attention to his suffering and death. As part of these celebrations we also hear particular interpretations, perhaps without being aware that there may be other valid but different interpretations. Atonement and sacrifice, for example, receive lots of emphasis. We rarely hear that John's Gospel does not use the language of sacrifice or ransom but rather epiphany. Jesus's crucifixion is the manifestation of God, part of his "hour" of glorification.

---

1. Arthur J. Dewey, "Can We Let Jesus Die?" in *The Once and Future Faith*, ed. Karen Armstrong et al. (Santa Rosa, CA: Polebridge, 2001), 144.

Popular piety has developed various themes from Scripture and tradition regarding both Jesus's suffering and our own. Let this verse from the traditional song "How Great Thou Art" serve as an example: "And when I think that God, His Son not sparing, sent Him to die, I scarce can take it in that on the cross, my burden gladly bearing, He bled and died to take away my sin! Then sings my soul, my Savior God, to Thee; how great Thou art, how great Thou art!"

Many of us have heard popular piety's various interpretations of human suffering. "It is God's punishment for sin." "It is a way for God to test us." "God never gives us more than we can handle." These and other similar statements clearly are attempts to respond to the mystery of suffering, to satisfy the human urge to ask "Why?" Much more must be said about all this in the following pages of this book.

Our World and the Arts

Another source in the mystery of suffering is the daily newspaper or the evening newscast. Worldwide communications keep us informed about all the most recent tragedies: the latest outbreak of genocide, the continuing spread of diseases, another earthquake, an environmental disaster. The list goes on and on. We meet the people and hear their stories every day.

Here are a few examples from the news the day this text was prepared for publication. (1) The leaders of the United States and North Korea threaten nuclear war. (2) Twenty million people are facing famine in Africa; more than one million severely malnourished children will likely die in the next few months. (3) Two mountain climbers die in an accident. (4) Hundreds of migrants are illegally crossing the border into Canada. (5) Man and transgender wife sue local company for bias. (6) Second man arrested in zoo knife attack.

Because suffering is such a central part of our lives, it has also become a favorite topic of the arts. So, along with the real pain of human life, we also confront suffering in all forms of artistic presentations: television, music, novels, plays, paintings, sculptures.

Many of the most popular TV shows, for example, are centered in hospitals, police departments, and courtrooms. The dramas base their stories on violence, murder, and sickness. Other shows focus on the difficulties and struggles of personal relationships.

Many different paths, indeed, lead to the mystery of suffering. Its reality is without doubt, always present. The human response to suffering usually includes the "Why?" question. For believers, suffering also raises questions about God. How could God permit or even cause suffering? How can we combine belief in a just and powerful God with the reality of suffering? This question expresses the ancient issue of *theodicy*, or looking to justify the ways of God.

The Law of Retribution

Such a search became an urgent activity of the Jewish people in exile in Babylon in the sixth century BCE. They faced serious suffering and profound questioning: How and why did God's chosen people end up in exile, with their land occupied and their temple destroyed? Their answer, expressed in Deuteronomy and developed in the Deuteronomistic writings, has shaped major sections of the Bible. In a way, the response is very simple: obey God, and you will be blessed; disobey God, and you will be punished. The people in exile, then, interpreted this political-social event as God's punishment for their failure to follow the covenant faithfully.

Here are some typical texts that express this basic conviction, called the Law of Retribution. Though describing an earlier time, the texts were written during the exile and so must be interpreted in that context—namely, that the people now experience the loss of their land because they did not follow the law. Their only hope is that, once their sin has been removed, Israel can again flourish.

> Now this is the commandment—the statutes and the ordinances—that the Lord your God charged me to teach you to observe in the land that you are about to cross into and occupy, so that you and your children and your children's children may fear the Lord your God all the days of your life, and keep all his decrees and his commandments that I am commanding you, so that your days may be long. Hear therefore, O Israel, and observe them diligently, so that it may go well with you, and so that you may multiply greatly in a land flowing with milk and honey, as the Lord, the God of your ancestors, has promised you. (Deut 6:1–3)

> See, I have set before you today life and prosperity, death and adversity. If you obey the commandments of the Lord your God that I am commanding you today, by loving the Lord your God, walking in his ways, and observing his commandments, decrees, and ordinances, then you shall live and become numerous, and the Lord your God will bless you in the land that you are entering to possess. But if your heart turns away and you do not hear, but are led astray to bow down to other gods and serve them, I declare to you today that you shall perish; you shall not live long in the land that you are crossing the Jordan to enter and possess. (Deut 30:15–18)

> But just as all the good things that the Lord your God promised concerning you have been fulfilled for you, so the Lord will bring upon you all the bad things, until he has destroyed you from this good land that the Lord your God has given you. If you transgress the covenant of the Lord your God, which he enjoined on

you, and go and serve other gods, and bow down to them, then the anger of the Lord will be kindled against you, and you shall perish quickly from the good land that he has given to you. (Josh 23:15–16)

Then the Israelites did what was evil in the sight of the Lord and worshiped the Ba'als; and they abandoned the Lord, the God of their ancestors, who had brought them out of the land of Egypt. . . . So the anger of the Lord was kindled against Israel, and he gave them over to plunderers who plundered them, and he sold them into the power of their enemies all around, so that they could no longer withstand their enemies . . . and they were in great distress. Then the Lord raised up judges, who delivered them out of the power of those who plundered them. (Judg 2:11–16)

Judges tempers Joshua by showing that, despite what God says in Joshua, God is free to act differently and does—by forgiving. God overlooks sinfulness and raises up new leaders—just what the people in exile need to hear!

This sense that suffering is God's punishment for sin certainly influenced the Christian tradition. We have already considered some of the texts that suggested Jesus's suffering and death as atonement for sin. The rich, symbolic texts of Revelation offer another example.

Then I heard a loud voice from the temple telling the seven angels, "Go and pour out on the earth the seven bowls of the wrath of God." So the first angel went and poured his bowl on the earth, and a foul and painful sore came on those who had the mark of the beast and who worshiped its image. . . . The third angel poured his bowl into the rivers and the springs of water, and they became blood. And I heard the angel of the waters say, "You are just, O Holy One, who are and were, for you have judged these things; because they shed the blood of saints and prophets, you have given them blood to drink. It is what they deserve!" . . . The fifth angel poured his bowl on the throne of the beast, and its kingdom was plunged into darkness; people gnawed their tongues in agony, and cursed the God of heaven because of their pains and sores, and they did not repent of their deeds. . . . The seventh angel poured his bowl into the air, and a loud voice came out of the temple, from the throne, saying, "It is done!" And there came flashes of lightning, rumblings, peals of thunder, and a violent earthquake, such as had not occurred since people were upon the earth, so violent was the earthquake. The great city was split into three parts, and the cities of the nations fell. God remembered great Babylon and gave her the wine-cup of the fury of his wrath. (Rev 16:1–2, 4–6, 10–11, 17–19)

Holding together sin and suffering continues to shape religious worldviews and to offer a reason for suffering. Many everyday examples can be found in newspaper accounts of disasters: following a hurricane in an East Coast town, a local resident stated that the storm was God's call to the people to change their lives; after both a terrorist attack and later a tornado, a resident of a Midwestern city concluded that the townspeople must be doing something wrong; peasants in a central American country judged their many earthquakes to be God's punishment for sin. At times, the conviction is expressed in judgmental and prejudiced (and uninformed) comments such as, "AIDS is God's punishment for homosexual sin."

Certainly, the belief about suffering as punishment goes beyond Judaism and Christianity. When an earthquake and landslides devastated parts of Turkey, the people (Muslims) concluded that it was God's punishment for their impiety. After a total eclipse of the sun in Africa, tribal healers warned that the ancestors were not happy with a nation that had abandoned traditional African values and that as retribution they would bring more conflict to the country. Perhaps Deuteronomy simply tapped into a deep human instinct.

Other Views

Despite this massive emphasis on suffering as punishment for sin, there have been notable people who have disagreed, for example, Job, Qoheleth, and Jesus. While we usually think of the book of Job as being about suffering (and it is), the underlying issue is the religious worldview. Job disagrees with Deuteronomy. The whole book is a challenge to the Deuteronomistic conviction that suffering is God's punishment for sin. Job suffers but claims his innocence (and, given the story's format, we know this to be true).

Qoheleth also challenges the Law of Retribution by appealing to his experience. Qoheleth (the book in the Bible is called Ecclesiastes, the Greek translation of Qoheleth, meaning "the leader of the assembly") states that he has seen "righteous people who perish in their righteousness, and there are wicked people who prolong their life in evil-doing" (Eccl 7:15). Qoheleth questions the wisdom tradition's tendency to limit God's freedom with its strict application of the Law of Retribution. He emphasizes instead divine sovereignty.

In his day, Jesus also disagreed with the common conviction. As described by John's Gospel, Jesus explicitly rejects the belief in the scene of the man born blind (John 9:1–41). When the disciples ask, "Rabbi, who sinned, this man or his parents, that he was born blind?," Jesus responds, "Neither this man nor his parents sinned; he was born blind so that God's works might be revealed in him." Typically, Jesus expresses a new vision, turning people's expectations and convictions upside down. Similar surprises can be found in the Sermon on the Mount and in the parables.

One section of the Sermon on the Mount is particularly enlightening. Jesus says, "You have heard that it was said, 'An eye for an eye and a tooth for a tooth.' But I say to you, Do not resist an evildoer. But if anyone strikes you on the right cheek, turn the other also" (Matt 5:38–39). He adds several other examples. In *The Powers That Be*, Walter Wink's creative and convincing interpretation of these examples denies that Jesus is endorsing passivity but rather is urging an original and nonviolent response that upsets the oppressive power structure. Jesus's vision of the reign of God includes a different way of valuing relationships both with oppressors and enemies, and with God.[2]

Jesus goes on, "But I say to you, Love your enemies and pray for those who persecute you, so that you may be children of your Father in heaven; for he makes his sun rise on the evil and on the good, and sends rain on the righteous and on the unrighteous" (Matt 5:44–45). Jesus calls for remarkable behavior and then gives the reason: so that members of the community can truly be children of God. Indeed, this God goes beyond the ordinary bounds of justice; this God is a God of the just and the unjust. This God does not limit divine love only to the good but also showers it on the evil.

Jesus's surprising understanding of God is also expressed in the parables. Luke presents the story of the "prodigal son," emphasizing Jesus's desire to find the lost (the other two parables in this chapter are about the lost sheep and the lost coin) and illustrating God's concern for sinners—not with anger or punishment but reconciliation and love.

> But while he [the son] was still far off, his father saw him and was filled with compassion; he ran and put his arms around him and kissed him. . . . But the father said to his slaves, "Quickly, bring out a robe—the best one—and put it on him; put a ring on his fin-

2. Walter Wink, *The Powers That Be* (New York: Doubleday, 1998), 98–111.

ger and sandals on his feet. And get the fatted calf and kill it, and let us eat and celebrate." (Luke 15:20–23)

Developing and Questioning Tradition

Some of Jesus's disciples, however, were not able to sustain this new worldview. In the face of Jesus's own horrible death, they appealed to images of sacrifice and atonement as a way of interpretation. As a result, violence and a demanding God returned to the center of the tradition, as we already considered in some of the Gospels, the writings of Paul, and Revelation.

Throughout the centuries, human beings have always combined religious tradition, philosophical systems, cultural influences, and their own experience in their attempts to find meaning in Jesus's suffering and their own. As believers in the twenty-first century, we hear these many different interpretations, often without appreciating fully the past cultural influences and the philosophical nuances. What develops in our religious practices and popular piety, then, may easily include convictions that are theologically inadequate or even problematic. (For a more detailed study of this phenomenon, see Anthony Tambasco's *A Theology of Atonement and Paul's Vision of Christianity*.) For example, some of the biblical images themselves (see Hebrews), and especially later theories of atonement, can easily lead to the conclusion that God demanded Jesus's suffering and death. Only an infinite sacrifice can make up for an infinite offense. Jesus's purpose in life is to suffer and die for our sins. Then we can view our own suffering in light of this conviction, joining our suffering with Jesus's suffering, "offering it up" and judging it to be redemptive.

Surely at one level it is very consoling to think that Jesus loved us so much that he suffered and died for us. Another question, however, must be asked in this explanation: What does this theory say about God the Father? As understood in popular piety, this God appears angry, demanding, even blood-thirsty. While those characteristics may have fit political powers of many ages, they certainly do not fit the God revealed by Jesus. Often this final issue—what this view says about God—is not articulated. We stop with Jesus's willingness to suffer and die for us. We must, however, take the final step and ask if the theory really fits the God described by Jesus in his life and parables.

Another reason for questioning the view that implies an angry, vindictive God is simply common sense. Our experience of good parents finds forgiveness, nourishment, compassion, and love. We know that there are parents who harm or even torture their children. We judge these actions to be evil. Certainly, we cannot speak of a good God who demands the Son's torture and suffering and death. Who could pray to that type of God?

Christian Scripture and tradition offer alternative interpretations not only for Jesus's suffering and death but also for the very purpose of his life. With these alternative interpretations come different possibilities for understanding and responding to our own suffering.

Appropriately, we start "in the beginning," with Jesus.

For Reflection, Prayer, and Discussion

In this chapter we have considered many different paths to suffering and a variety of interpretations of this profound human experience.

1. Gently recall some events of significant suffering in your life or your family's history. How did you and others respond? In what ways has the suffering in our world touched you?

2. How have the Scriptures helped or hindered your dealing with suffering? Prayerfully read the book of Job or the Sermon on the Mount.

3. How have you or a friend used the Law of Retribution? Were you satisfied?

2

The Life and Vision of Jesus

All theologies and interpretations must first be rooted in the events of Jesus's life and death. Before considering these various interpretations more closely, then, let's turn to the life of Jesus as the foundation for all that is to follow in this book. Jesus of Nazareth was born and grew to adulthood. He traveled through Galilee, revealing to people the "reign of God" in his words and deeds. He made his journey to Jerusalem, and there he was crucified (a terrible form of capital punishment used by the Romans who occupied Jesus's homeland).

Listening to the Scriptures

Almost all our knowledge of Jesus comes from the community that was founded on him. There are only a couple of brief references to Jesus from secular sources, for example, the Roman historian Tacitus. Thus, we can discover Jesus's experience only by listening to what the Christian community said about him in the Scriptures. And the Scriptures, of course, are accounts of faith. The New Testament, like the Old Testament, has a purpose: to tell us of God's action in the world, not to give an exact historical or scientific account of events. In telling the story of Jesus, the Christian community included its faith perspective in the very details of the story.

A few dates will be helpful in interpreting the stories about Jesus. The four Gospels were not written down until long after Jesus's death (about 30 CE). After his death and resurrection, those who had come to believe in him began telling their story to others. These stories recalled teachings and events in Jesus's life. Some of these accounts may have been written; others were handed on orally. The first Gospel we have today (Mark) was not written until some forty years after Jesus's death—that is, about 70 CE. In the next ten to twenty years, the Gospels of Matthew and Luke were written. Both are based on Mark's Gospel together with other sources. John's Gospel wasn't written in its present form until the end of the first century. The oldest New Testament writings are Paul's authentic letters, composed in the 50s and 60s CE.

As we turn to the Gospels to reflect on Jesus's life, then, we must deal with various layers of Christian experience and composition. The top layer is the Gospels, which are edited, rewritten, and theologically interpreted accounts about Jesus. The middle layer is an oral and written tradition made up of stories and anecdotes remembered by a particular community and handed on in a creative tradition shaped by community concerns. Finally, at the bottom is the material out of which a profile of the historical Jesus can be constructed.

These three stages of Gospel formation are clearly described in "The Historical Truth of the Gospels," an *Instruction* of the

Roman Pontifical Biblical Commission approved by Pope Paul VI in 1964. (It was Pope Pius XII, in 1943, who first supported the use of modern methods of scriptural analysis.) The church's teaching reminds us, then, that the Gospels are not literal accounts of the ministry of Jesus but include the interpretations and adaptations of the second and third stages. Perhaps the image of "double exposure" can help us appreciate the layers present in the Gospels, which are faith proclamations about Jesus addressed to the concerns of a particular community forty to sixty years after Jesus's death.

Our View of Jesus

One caution: Many of us already hold firm convictions about the life of Jesus. We may need to work at hearing what is being said here. Certain presuppositions and conclusions may be different!

One of these convictions is a central element of the Christian faith: the belief that Jesus was both divine and human. This conviction is clearly expressed in the New Testament. We must remember, of course, that the Gospels were written from a post-resurrection perspective. The new insight and understanding that result from the resurrection experience color the way the stories are told—particularly since their very purpose is expressing faith! Thus, the divinity of Jesus is affirmed throughout the Gospels, even to his preexistence as the Word (see John 1:1–18).

For those of us who come almost two thousand years later, faith in Jesus's divinity is taken for granted. Indeed, many of us may find it easier to believe that Jesus was God than to accept that he was truly a human.

But in our attempt to appreciate Jesus's life and ministry,

we must try to get behind these faith statements to the experiences themselves. We want to know what happened to Jesus and what led his disciples to claim that he was God in the first place.

Our own experience of Jesus is just about the opposite of the disciples' experience of him. The disciples first encountered a human being, Jesus of Nazareth. Only gradually—indeed, not until after the resurrection—would they recognize and proclaim his divinity. To appreciate fully Jesus's and the disciples' experiences, we must try to follow that same path.

Of course we are dealing here with mystery, a human being who is also divine. While we cannot really explain what it means to be divine, we do know what it means to be human. So we can start at this point in our pondering of Jesus's life. Jesus was human. He had to face the same basic realities of life that we do: love and friendship, discouragement and loss, ignorance and pain, joy and trust. Jesus had to eat and drink; he had to learn and figure out how he was to live his life.

Yes, this implies that Jesus did not know the future. To be truly human, Jesus had to search for meaning as we all do. The Christian faith proclaims that Jesus was indeed truly and fully human (in every way except sin). Therefore, whatever we know of our human condition we can safely attribute to Jesus.

How, then, does Jesus's divinity fit in? Perhaps by not interfering with his being fully human. For any interference—such as divine foreknowledge, explicitly operative in Jesus's human consciousness—would rob Jesus of his humanity. He would not then truly be like one of us. True, the Scriptures seem to tell the story otherwise and emphasize his divinity; that is why it is so important to remember *when* they were written (after the resurrection) and *why* (to proclaim Jesus as Lord and Savior).

Another dimension of Jesus's life was his experience of religion. The story of the people of Israel was Jesus's story. As he grew, Jesus listened to and prayed with the Hebrew Scriptures. He pondered the lives of Abraham and Moses, of Jeremiah and Isaiah. Their God was Jesus's God—a God who continued to be active in people's lives, freeing and choosing and calling them back to the covenant. This Jewish context, then, nurtured Jesus's knowledge of and relationship with God.

We can also gain insight into Jesus's experience by looking at Jesus's activities and teachings as described in the Gospels. In attempting to appreciate the heart of his life, we will pay special attention to Jesus's faithful and loving relationship with God and to Jesus's understanding of the reign of God.

Relationship with God

Scripture scholars have helped us to appreciate the significance of Jesus's relationship with God, whom he addressed as "Father" and perhaps even "*Abba.*" Some scholars say that Jesus chose this word that small children used to address their fathers. *Abba* is best translated "Daddy"; it conveys a sense of childlike simplicity and familiarity.

Other Scripture scholars have recently described a different image for understanding Jesus's relationship with God: that of a patron. Appreciating the cultural world of the first century suggests this alternative interpretation, which implies a mature, personal relationship with the one who empowers, with special emphasis on trust, responsibility, and fidelity.

Although offering different emphases, these images are important for our consideration of Jesus's experience because they point to a very profound relationship between God and Jesus. How did it develop? We have no way of answering in detail, but we can assume that this bond developed gradually as Jesus lived life, heard the Hebrew Scriptures, asked himself about his own response to God, listened to John the Baptist, and began his own prophetic ministry, taking time to be alone and to pray. The God of Abraham, Isaac, Jacob, Moses, Isaiah, and Jeremiah was Father to Jesus.

We catch another glimpse into Jesus's experience of God in the parables. One of the most helpful is Luke 15:11–32, often called the parable of the prodigal son. This parable about the possibility of reconciliation (which we briefly considered in chap. 1) is better described, however, as the parable of the forgiving father. The details are familiar: the younger son demands his inheritance, leaves home, spends all the money, and finally returns to his father's house, asking to be treated as a servant. Notice the actions of the father: he allows his son freedom even to waste the inheritance; he watches for his return; he forgives the son without any bitterness, throwing a party to celebrate; and he goes out to console the angry older brother. In this parable Jesus is telling us a lot about his own experience of God. *Abba* is a loving, forgiving, gentle parent. Jesus evidently feels very close to this personal God, a God who reaches out to all, both those who wander away and those who stay at home.

If we look closely at the events and teachings of Jesus's life, we see that Jesus focused his energies neither on himself nor on the church. Jesus's whole life was directed to the reign of God.

The Reign of God

The reign of God is a central image in the Gospels. Simply put, the reign of God means that God's power is at work in a particular situation. God's saving presence is found there. The reign (also called kingdom or sovereignty) of God does not imply a particular place or time; it is present whenever and wherever God's loving presence is manifested. Therefore the reign of God may exist in individual persons, in institutions, and in the whole world. The miracles of Jesus are symbols of God's reign breaking into our world, of healing and salvation overcoming brokenness and sin.

Let's look at one powerful example given in the Gospels. For the people of Israel, leprosy had become not only a medical problem but also a ritual impurity. The people considered the disease to be divine punishment and feared that the community would also suffer if the leper was not forced outside the town.

Jesus not only rejects the judgment but also crosses the boundaries of purity laws to touch the alienated. Mark's Gospel describes the scene this way: "A leper came to him begging him, and kneeling he said to him, 'If you choose, you can make me clean.' Moved with pity, Jesus stretched out his hand and touched him, and said to him, 'I do choose. Be made clean!' Immediately the leprosy left him, and he was made clean" (Mark 1:40–42). With a simple but profound touch, Jesus breaks down barriers, challenges customs and laws that alienate, and embodies his convictions about the inclusive meaning of the reign of God. This dramatic touch is also described in the other two Synoptic Gospels in Matthew 8:1–4 and Luke 5:12–16.

This event reveals not only Jesus's care for an individual in need but also his concern about structures of society. Jesus steps across the boundaries separating the unclean and actually touches the leper. In doing so, Jesus enters into the leper's isolation and becomes unclean. Human care and compassion, not cultural values of honor and shame, direct Jesus's action. He calls into question the purity code, which alienates and oppresses people already in need. Indeed, this encounter with the leper is one example of how Jesus reaches out to the marginal people in Jewish society, whether they be women, the possessed, or lepers.

Jesus used parables to speak about the reign of God. Although he thus risked being misunderstood, Jesus allowed his listeners to make the connection between what he was talking about and what they were already expecting. He usually upset many of their preconceived notions of God's righteousness and power. Yet he took a chance that his words would touch the people in their depths and that they would act upon this discovery. He did so because he believed that the reign of God, so evident in his own experience, could—and would—be recognized by others.

At times Jesus began his parables with the statement, "The reign of God is like . . ." At other times, this statement is only implied. In Luke 8:4–15, for instance, Jesus simply begins, "A farmer went out to sow some seed" and goes on to describe the different types of ground on which the seed fell. Part of *our* need in hearing this parable is to recognize that Jesus is describing very poor farming techniques. His hearers at the time, of course, knew that; they also knew that even the best techniques of the day produced about sevenfold. But in the parable the rich soil produces a hundredfold. Jesus is telling his listeners how surprising God's reign is, how overflowing in goodness—not sevenfold but a hundredfold!

A similar parable can also be misunderstood because we do not know specifics from Jesus's day. In Luke 13:20–21, Jesus describes a woman mixing yeast into three measures of flour. Most of us miss the heart of Jesus's teaching because we do not know that three "measures" of flour is enough for fifty pounds of bread! Years ago in an *I Love Lucy* episode, Lucy was baking bread, and this huge loaf just kept rising and coming out of the oven, finally pinning her against the kitchen wall. The exaggeration of the Lucy show expresses the heart of the parable. The reign of God is full of joy and surprise and goodness.

Because of Jesus's intimate relationship with God, Jesus experienced the presence of the reign in and through his own life. And what he tried to tell others in his parables is that they could experience this reign too!

Another section of Luke that provides rich insight into Jesus's experience of God's loving and saving presence is what we commonly know as the Sermon on the Mount (although the location in Luke's Gospel is level ground—see Luke 6:17–49; cf. Matt 5:1–7:29). In this collection of Jesus's teachings, we discover some of the surprise and goodness of the reign of God: the hungry will be satisfied; those who weep now will laugh; those who are poor will be part of the reign. The Sermon also gives other characteristics of life in the reign of God: love of enemies, generosity, compassion, forgiveness, humility, and authentic action. And, as is typical of Luke's Gospel, we also hear about the dangers of wealth and complacency.

Baptism and Mission

We can also deepen our appreciation of Jesus's life and vision by looking at events of his life such as his baptism (Luke 3:1–22). The conclusion of the baptism story states: "Now when all the people were baptized, and when Jesus also had been baptized and was praying, the heaven was opened and the Holy Spirit descended upon him in bodily form like a dove. And a voice came from heaven, 'You are my Son, the Beloved; with you I am well pleased'" (Luke 3:21–22). Did the sky really part, and did a voice boom from heaven? That is, of course, the wrong question. The Scriptures were not written to give this kind of information. Although we cannot say that it definitely never happened, our experience indicates that the sky does not open, the Holy Spirit is not a bird, and voices do not suddenly speak from the heavens.

We can and do, however, experience an awareness of our mission in life—our vocation. So it is likely that Luke is trying to describe with symbols Jesus's early sense of his own mission and of his special relationship with God. Such an understanding clearly fits with what we have been discussing in this chapter: the true humanity of Jesus and his intimate relationship with God.

Luke continues to develop the picture of Jesus's identity and mission in the keynote address in Nazareth.

> Then Jesus, filled with the power of the spirit, returned to Galilee, and a report about him spread through all the surrounding country. He began to teach in their synagogues and was praised by everyone. When he came to Nazareth, where he had been brought up, he went to the synagogue on the Sabbath day, as was his custom. He stood up to read, and the scroll of the prophet Isaiah was given to him. He unrolled the scroll and found the place where it was written:

> "The Spirit of the Lord is upon me,
> because he has anointed me
> to bring good news to the poor.
> He has sent me to proclaim release to the captives
> and recovery of sight to the blind,
> to let the oppressed go free,
> to proclaim the year of the Lord's favor."

> And he rolled up the scroll, gave it back to the attendant, and sat down. The eyes of all in the synagogue were fixed on him. Then he began to say to them. "Today this scripture has been fulfilled in your hearing." (Luke 4:14–21)

This marvelous and powerful scene is rich with statements about Jesus's identity and mission, presenting the heart of the gospel. Scripture scholars help us to appreciate Luke's creativity as artist and as theologian. Writing his Gospel many years after the death and resurrection of Jesus, Luke, of course, was not intending an exact historical account but rather a proclamation of faith. He wanted to share his community's experience and commitment and vision. So he felt free to rearrange his primary source, Mark's Gospel, by moving this scene to the very beginning of Jesus's public ministry. Luke's creativity is also found within the text itself as he weaves together selections from several different chapters of Isaiah and omits some other points. As it stands, this text would not be found on a synagogue scroll. Luke acts as artist in order to be preacher.

And this passage is truly a keynote, establishing the basic themes of Luke's Gospel. Jesus, the anointed one (the Messiah, the Christ), teaches and heals and proclaims the presence of God's reign. Jesus is the fulfillment of God's promises for the hungry, the sick, and the imprisoned.

Indeed, Luke's Gospel goes on to describe many examples of Jesus teaching and healing the poor, including Peter's mother-in-law and the leper. Then, when some disciples of John the Baptist ask Jesus, "Are you the one who is to come?," Jesus replies, "Go and tell John what you have seen and heard: the blind receive their sight, the lame walk, the lepers are cleansed, the deaf hear, the dead are raised, the poor have good news brought to them" (Luke 7:19, 21–22). God's reign is breaking into the world through Jesus.

Birth and Death

Since this chapter's understanding of the life, vision, and ministry of Jesus may be less familiar to some readers (scholars name it "Christology from below"), it may be helpful also to consider Jesus's birth and death.

Only two sources in the New Testament describe the birth of Jesus: Luke is one (1:1–2:52), and Matthew is the other (1:1–2:23). But the two stories are very, very different in their details. Because most of us have combined the two stories in our hearts and minds, we realize these differences only by looking carefully at the two accounts. Matthew focuses on Joseph, has Mary and Joseph living in Bethlehem, and includes the magi and the flight into Egypt. Luke focuses on Mary, has Mary and Joseph living in Nazareth (going to Bethlehem only for the Roman census), and includes the shepherds and a peaceful visit to Jerusalem. Once again, we must avoid asking the wrong question: Which way did it happen?

In his extensive study of the infancy narratives, *The Birth of the Messiah*, Raymond Brown emphasizes that what is important is the religious message of the stories. (For a much shorter account, see Brown's *An Adult Christ at Christmas*.) What is this message? Brown claims it is twofold: to proclaim the identity of Jesus as truly God and truly human, and to show how Jesus is linked to and fulfills the Hebrew Scriptures. Brown states that each infancy narrative is, in fact, the whole gospel in miniature: the full identity of Jesus (divine and human) is revealed, and this good news is shared with others and accepted by some (shepherds, magi, Simeon, Anna) but rejected by others (Herod the king, the chief priests and scribes). Understood in this way, the message of the story of Jesus's birth affirms this chapter's insights into the experience of Jesus and in no way contradicts them.

Let's now look at the other end of Jesus's life: his passion, death, and resurrection. As with the infancy accounts, we tend to combine the different passion narratives in our hearts and minds. Still, there are significant differences in the four portraits. For example, Mark describes Jesus as abandoned by his disciples, rejected by the crowd, and seemingly forsaken by his God. But John describes Jesus as being in control, freely laying down his life, and dying in a sovereign and life-giving manner. (See Raymond Brown's *The Death of the Messiah* for a detailed study; for a much shorter comparison, see his *A Crucified Christ in Holy Week*.) Thus, even the passion accounts, while rooted in a historical fact (the crucifixion), are stories of faith in which theology, not biography, determines which events are narrated. (We will consider this point in more detail in the next chapter.)

What, then, as an example, are some of the specific brush-strokes in Luke's portrait (Luke 22:1–23:56) of the passion? Luke invites his hearers not so much to adore Jesus as Son of God (John's portrait), learn about him (Matthew's), or look on the scene in overwhelming sorrow (Mark's), but simply to be with Jesus. Luke invites the hearer to become another Simon of Cyrene helping Jesus carry his cross, another Peter recognizing weakness, another good thief expressing hope.

Luke's passion story continues to emphasize the same characteristics and experiences of Jesus found throughout the Gospel. Jesus is not overwhelmed with fear and agony but prays in the garden and calmly faces death, just as he steadfastly journeyed toward Jerusalem in the prior narrative. Jesus heals the high priest's slave as he healed so many during his ministry. Jesus consoles the "daughters of Jerusalem" and forgives those who crucified him in the same way he described mercy and tenderness in his parables and expressed them in his actions. Finally, as he dies, Jesus continues to express his profound trust in God; his last words are, "Father, into your hands, I commend my spirit" (Luke 23:46b).

This trust is a striking contrast to the abandonment expressed in Mark 15:34 and Matthew 27:47: "My God, my God, why have you forsaken me?" It is different from the sovereign control and triumph expressed in John: "After this, when Jesus knew that all was now finished, he said (in order to fulfill the scripture) . . . " (19:28), and "It is finished" (19:30). Jesus's faithful, loving relationship with God sustains him even in death.

But the passion and death are only the beginning of Jesus's glorification. The resurrection completes this central event. In the descriptions of the resurrection we find much symbolic language: dazzling lights, sudden appearances, a mysterious inability to recognize Jesus but then ecstatic joy with the recognition, and a sudden fading away. All this reminds us that the resurrection is a different kind of reality, not the same kind of historical event as the crucifixion.

The resurrection is an experience in faith, known and proclaimed by the disciples but denied by unbelievers. The disciples experienced Jesus as alive in a new way. His presence transformed them and their world. How else can one describe such an experience except with symbolic language?

The resurrection can be understood as God's affirmation of Jesus's faithfulness. His trusting, loving relationship is now confirmed by *Abba*'s power that raises Jesus to new life. The definitive triumph of life over death takes place in Jesus's resurrection.

Implications for Suffering

What does Jesus's life and teaching tell us about his view of suffering? At least three points: (1) Jesus rejected the conviction that suffering is the punishment for sin; (2) Jesus resisted suffering and its personal and social causes, and he is frequently described healing persons; and (3) Jesus expressed a profound trust in a loving, compassionate, and present God. As we saw in chapter 1, Matthew's Jesus in the Sermon on the Mount describes God as showering God's rain (and love and life) on evil persons as well as good ones. Similarly, John's Jesus heals the blind man and rejects the Deuteronomistic worldview. Many other stories tell of Jesus healing the blind and the sick. Throughout his public ministry, Jesus boldly proclaims God's loving presence, takes time to nurture his own relationship with *Abba*, and acts in light of and teaches about trusting this God. Another example from the Sermon on the Mount emphasizes this trust:

> Therefore I tell you, do not worry about your life, what you will eat or what you will drink, or about your body, what you will wear. Is not life more than food, and the body more than clothing? Look at the birds of the air; they neither sow nor reap nor gather into barns, and yet your heavenly Father feeds them. Are you not of more value than they? And can any of you by worrying add a single hour to your span of life? And why do you worry about clothing? Consider the lilies of the field, how they grow; they neither toil nor spin, yet I tell you, even Solomon in all his glory was not clothed like one of these. But if God so clothes the grass of the field, which is alive today and tomorrow is thrown into the oven, will he not much more clothe you—you of little faith? Therefore do not worry, saying, "What will we eat?" or "What will we drink?" or "What will we wear?" For it is the Gentiles who strive for all these things; and indeed your heavenly Father knows that you need all these things. But strive first for

the kingdom of God and his righteousness, and all these things will be given to you as well. (Matt 6:25–33)

For Reflection, Prayer, and Discussion

In this chapter we have considered the life, vision, and ministry of Jesus, along with implications for suffering.

1. What scene from Jesus's life is your favorite? Why?

2. How do you look for the presence of the reign of God in your life? What are its main characteristics?

3. What is your reaction to the chapter's description of Jesus's view of suffering? What questions or insights does it suggest?

3

Jesus's Death and Its Interpretations

Then Jesus went about all the cities and villages, teaching in their synagogues, and proclaiming the good news of the kingdom, and curing every disease and every sickness. When he saw the crowds, he had compassion for them, because they were harassed and helpless, like sheep without a shepherd. (Matt 9:35, 36)

The life and teachings of Jesus highlight the healing presence of a God of love and life. In the end, however, Jesus suffered a horrible execution. Not only did his followers try to make sense of this death, they also confronted death in their communities—at times violent death. So they searched for meaning, looking for light. Naturally, these followers of Jesus turned to their Hebrew Scriptures along with the person and teachings of Jesus.

Despite the Gospels' differences in describing Jesus's passion and death, there is one coherent and consecutive story running through the various versions. Also, the Gospels share, of course, a common viewpoint—the post-resurrection perspective. Transformed by the resurrection, the followers of Jesus proclaimed his story. Thus, as we saw in the beginning of chapter 2, the Gospels contain various layers and interpretations, woven together in all the texts, including the stories of Jesus's passion and death.

The Innocent Sufferer

For many years, Judaism had wrestled with the issue of martyrdom, the death of righteous persons. Especially its later literature (the wisdom and apocalyptic writings) developed a typical structure for the "tale of the innocent sufferer." Arthur J. Dewey summarizes this structure in his careful study, "Can We Let Jesus Die?" He writes:

> In this Tale the actions and claims of an innocent person provoke his opponents to conspire against him. This leads to an accusation, trial, condemnation, and ordeal. In some instances this results in his shameful death. The hero of the story reacts characteristically, expressing his innocence, frustration, or trust in prayer, while there are also various reactions to his fate by characters in the tale. Either at the brink of death or in death itself the innocent one is rescued and vindicated. This vindication entails the exaltation and acclamation of the hero as well as the reaction and punishment of his opponents.[1]

We can find this type of understanding of the death of righteous persons in Wisdom 2–5 and in the stirring story of the seven brothers and their mother in 2 Maccabees 7. The Psalms and Prophets also contribute to this portrait of the innocent sufferer.

Dewey goes on to show the many connections between the

---

1. Arthur Dewey, "Can We Let Jesus Die?," in *The Once and Future Faith*, ed. Karen Armstrong et al. (Santa Rosa, CA: Polebridge, 2001), 147.

Gospels and these sections of the Hebrew Scriptures. He points out that the Gospels not only borrowed the structure of the "tale of the innocent sufferer" to form the passion story, but the Gospels also applied the same interpretation to Jesus. Dewey also argues that the early communities used some of the content of the Hebrew Scriptures to construct the passion accounts.[2]

Because this idea of the martyr is so significant, let's take some time to look at examples of all these points. Here are a few excerpts from the book of Wisdom (written in the first century BCE).

> Let us lie in wait for the righteous man, because he is inconvenient to us and opposes our actions; he reproaches us for our sins against the law, and accuses us of sins against our training. He professes to have knowledge of God, and calls himself a child of the Lord. (Wis 2:12–13)

> If the righteous man is God's child, he will help him, and will deliver him from the hand of his adversaries. Let us test him with insult and torture, so that we may find out how gentle he is, and make trial of his forbearance. Let us condemn him to a shameful death, for, according to what he says, he will be protected. (Wis 2:18–20)

> But the souls of the righteous are in the hand of God, and no torment will ever touch them. In the eyes of the foolish they seem to have died, and their departure was thought to be a disaster, and their going from us to be their destruction; but they are at peace. (Wis 3:1–3)

> The righteous who have died will condemn the ungodly who are living, and youth that is quickly perfected will condemn the prolonged old age of the unrighteous. For they will see the end of the

---

2. Dewey, "Can We Let Jesus Die?," 148, 153–58; see also his book on how the death of Jesus was remembered, *Inventing the Passion: How the Death of Jesus Was Remembered* (Salem, OR: Polebridge, 2017).

wise, and will not understand what the Lord purposed for them, and for what he kept them safe. (Wis 4:16–17)

But the righteous live forever, and their reward is with the Lord; the Most High takes care of them. (Wis 5:15)

Second Maccabees 7 (from the second century BCE) describes the horrible executions of the brothers and their mother—and their remarkable faith.

The Lord God is watching over us and in truth has compassion on us, as Moses declared in his song that bore witness against the people to their faces, when he said, "And he will have compassion on his servants." (2 Macc 7:6)

You accursed wretch, you dismiss us from this present life, but the King of the universe will raise us up to an everlasting renewal of life, because we have died for his laws. (2 Macc 7:9)

One cannot but choose to die at the hands of mortals and to cherish the hope God gives of being raised again by him. But for you there will be no resurrection to life! (2 Macc 7:14)

Another example of the innocent sufferer is found in the apocalyptic book of Daniel (composed around 165 BCE). Apocalyptic literature reflects its roots in the experience of oppression by looking for rescue by some form of divine intervention. The righteous will be vindicated, then, when this intervention occurs, perhaps in the last judgment.

The book of Daniel addresses another crisis in Israel, the attempt by Antiochus IV Epiphanes to outlaw Jewish practices and to impose pagan religion. With symbols and visions (another characteristic of apocalyptic literature), Daniel uses stories about contests and conflicts in Babylon in the sixth century to speak to the real concerns of the second century.

At the center of these concerns was suffering and oppression. So the book of Daniel calls for fidelity and urges the people to trust that God will deliver them. On that day, the righteous Jews will be vindicated and evil rulers punished.

> At that time Michael, the great prince, the protector of your people, shall arise. There shall be a time of anguish, such as has never occurred since nations first came into existence. But at that time your people shall be delivered, everyone who is found written in the book. Many of those who sleep in the dust of the earth shall awake, some to everlasting life, and some to shame and everlasting contempt. Those who are wise shall shine like the brightness of the sky, and those who lead many to righteousness, like the stars forever and ever. (Dan 12:1–3)

This conviction is presented most dramatically in the third chapter of Daniel. Shadrach, Meshach, and Abednego are thrown into a blazing furnace because they refuse to worship a golden statue. However, they are not at all harmed, and they are delivered by God (3:1–30).

Details of Dying

As we already have seen in chapter 1, the Psalms and Prophets also provided the followers of Jesus a way to interpret and perhaps even describe his death. Here are only a few excerpts from many possible sources in the Psalms (collected over hundreds of years BCE).

> Many are the afflictions of the righteous,
> but the Lord rescues them from them all.
> He keeps all their bones;
> not one of them will be broken. (Ps 34:19–20)

> I keep the Lord always before me;
> because he is at my right hand, I shall not be moved.
> Therefore my heart is glad, and my soul rejoices;
> my body also rests secure.
> For you do not give me up to Sheol, or let your faithful one see

the Pit.
You show me the path of life.
In your presence there is fullness of joy;
in your right hand are pleasures forever. (Ps 16:8–11)

They gave me poison for food,
and for my thirst they gave me vinegar to drink. (Ps 69:21)

I can count all my bones.
They stare and gloat over me;
they divide my clothes among themselves,
and for my clothing they cast lots. (Ps 22:17–18)

My God, my God, why have you forsaken me? (Ps 22:1)

Into your hand I commit my spirit. (Ps 31:5)

Ransom and Sacrifice

Other themes in the Hebrew Scriptures along with civic and religious practices also led to different interpretations. In their world, these followers of Jesus knew about paying a ransom to free captives and slaves. In both Jewish devotions and others' devotions, the sacrifice of animals, crops, and other objects was very common. In the Jewish celebration of the Day of Atonement, two goats served as victims. One was driven out into the desert, symbolically taking with it the sins of the people. The other was killed, and its blood was poured out in the temple.

These sources clearly influenced some of the Gospels and other writings in the New Testament. Mark's Gospel states that the Son of Man came "to give his life as a ransom for many" (10:45). Paul's theology of the cross uses imagery of ransom and heroic sacrifice: "They are now justified by his [God's] grace as a gift, through the redemption that is in Christ Jesus, whom God put forward as a sacrifice of atonement by his blood, effective through faith" (Rom 3:24–25); "Christ redeemed us from the curse of the law by becoming a curse for us—for it is written, 'Cursed is everyone who hangs on a tree'" (Gal 3:13). And the letter to the Hebrews abounds in the language and images of atonement and sacrifice.

So it is important for us to appreciate the meaning of these frequently used themes of sacrifice, atonement, and expiation. Scholars tell us that what the Bible understands by these terms may be quite different from the understandings that many of us have. Our images probably have been distorted by later theologies and pieties (as we will see later in this chapter). For example, for the Hebrew people, blood symbolized life, not death. "For the life of the flesh is in the blood; and I have given it to you for making atonement for your lives on the altar; for, as life, it is the blood that makes atonement" (Lev 17:11). The blood of the sacrificed animal, then, symbolized the life of the person or community. Pouring the blood on the altar was a symbolic gesture, reuniting the life with God.

Similarly, the people in the Hebrew Scriptures were not attempting to appease a cruel and angry God by their sacrifices. The Scripture texts simply do not support such a view. Rather, the sacrifices were an expression of their desire for union with God, which included a sense of reconciliation and making up for sin.

In Israelite religion, sacrifice was the main form of worship. The most solemn sacrifice was the holocaust, in which the offering was completely burned, making the gift to God irrevocable. Another form was the communion sacrifice, a thanksgiving offering in which portions of the sacrifice were shared among God (by burning), the priest, and the person making the offering. Other forms included sacrifices of expiation, offered for individuals or the whole community to reestablish the covenant relationship with God broken by sin. Various directives, especially in Leviticus, spell out the details of these rituals.

Even while emphasizing these more positive meanings of sacrifice, most of the scholars pass over in silence the fact that the ritual still includes violence and the death of the sacrifice, dimensions that were foreign to Jesus's vision of the reign of God.

However, given the centrality of sacrifice and the harsh reality of Jesus's execution, it cannot be a complete surprise that followers of Jesus returned to the idea of sacrifice to interpret Jesus's death, despite Jesus's teachings. As a sacrifice of expiation, some of the followers stated, Jesus's blood was poured out to reestablish the covenant relationship broken by sin. "Then he took a cup, and after giving thanks he gave it to them, and all of them drank from it. He said to them, 'This is my blood of the covenant, which is poured out for many'" (Mark 14:23–24). Indeed, Jesus's blood achieved perfectly what the sacrifices on the Day of Atonement had prefigured.

> But when Christ came as a high priest of the good things that have come, then through the greater and perfect tent (not made with hands, that is, not of this creation), he entered once for all into the Holy Place, not with the blood of goats and calves, but with his own blood, thus obtaining eternal redemption. For if the blood of goats and bulls, with the sprinkling of the ashes of a heifer, sanctifies those who have been defiled so that their flesh is purified, how much more will the blood of Christ, who through the eternal Spirit offered himself without blemish to God, purify our conscience from dead works to worship the living God! (Heb 9:11–14)

Suffering Servant

Jesus's followers also developed a specific and unique perspective on sacrifice by using the "suffering servant" theme from

Isaiah. Judaism did not expect a suffering Messiah, but the early Christian community creatively put together the texts from Isaiah with the death of Jesus. As we saw in chapter 1, Isaiah's suffering servant theme includes the concept of vicarious suffering, that is, suffering for the sake of other persons.

The songs of the suffering servant are found in that part of Isaiah called "Second Isaiah"—the unknown prophet who lived with the people during the exile in Babylon in the sixth century BCE. (The first part of the book, chaps. 1–39, comes from Isaiah of Jerusalem, around 700 BCE.)

The people faced profound suffering, the destruction of Jerusalem, and then exile. They naturally asked why. Second Isaiah accepted the theory of retribution expressed in the Deuteronomist tradition, judging that the suffering was punishment for sin. But now the time of liberation was present, a time of a new exodus to return to Jerusalem. Through the sufferings of the servant, Israel's sins were forgiven and relationship with God was reestablished.

Who was the suffering servant? Scholars are not certain. Some suggest a collective interpretation—Israel or a particular part of the community. Others focus on an individual—a leader of the community or the author. The servant's identity remains unknown, but his suffering is understood in terms of sacrifice, atoning for sin, and reconciling with God.

The success of the early Christians' creativity in joining the suffering servant to Jesus is seen in how easily today's Christians link the two, interpreting Jesus as the servant. The Messiah, of course, was not supposed to be a suffering messiah. The facts of crucifixion and death jarred Jesus's followers into searching the Hebrew Scriptures for insight for proclaiming and interpreting this death.

Let's listen again to a few excerpts from the dramatic servant passages.

Surely he has borne our infirmities and carried our diseases; yet we accounted him stricken, struck down by God, and afflicted. But he was wounded for our transgressions, crushed for our iniquities; upon him was the punishment that made us whole, and by his bruises we are healed. All we like sheep have gone astray; we have all turned to our own way, and the Lord has laid on him the iniquity of us all. (Isa 53:4–6)

The Lord God has opened my ear, and I was not rebellious, I did not turn backward. I gave my back to those who struck me, and my cheeks to those who pulled out the beard; I did not hide my face from insult and spitting. (Isa 50:5–6).

More Details

The writings of other prophets have also contributed to the interpretation and description of Jesus's suffering and dying.

On that day, says the Lord God, I will make the sun go down at noon, and darken the earth in broad daylight. (Amos 8:9; ca. 750 BCE)

And I will pour out a spirit of compassion and supplication on the house of David and the inhabitants of Jerusalem, so that, when they look on the one whom they have pierced, they shall mourn for him, as one mourns for an only child, and weep bitterly over him, as one weeps over a first born. On that day the mourning in Jerusalem will be as great as the mourning for Hadad-rimmon in the plain of Megiddo. (Zech 12:10–11; this section dates to the third century BCE)

These relatively few examples help to give us a sense of how the Hebrew Scriptures were a rich resource for the followers of Jesus. Indeed, a variety of the perspectives and interpretations were incorporated into the New Testament texts: the vindication of the righteous martyr, the suffering servant, sacrifice, atonement, and expiation. As was noted in chapter 2, each evangelist develops a unique portrait of Jesus, even while incorporating some of these and other interpretations. (We will consider some of the other interpretations, not as well known in popular piety but still part of Scripture, in the next chapters.)

The Hebrew sources may have also provided some of the content for the passion stories. Remembering that the Gospels are faith proclamations first and not exact historical accounts, we may never be able to know with certainty all that was part of Jesus's passion. Many have argued for the historical accuracy of the passion narratives, but the argument is based on plausibility. As Dewey points out, "Although plausibility alone never gets beyond the possible, readers and scholars alike are wont to assume that what is seen in the text connects to an unseen 'fact.'"[3] Even our brief review of the Hebrew Scriptures reveals some remarkable similarities with the passion stories. So it seems best to rest comfortably with the "perhaps" and the "possible."

Similarly, we may never be able to know with certainty all that led to Jesus's death. Perhaps Jesus was killed, as many people suggest, as a result of his ministry, proclaiming the love and freedom of God's reign, reaching out to the poor and marginalized. We know that such deaths still occur today, for example, Martin Luther King Jr., the four churchwomen in El Salvador, and the six Jesuits from the University of Central America. Perhaps he was simply seized and eliminated by the oppressive

---

3. Dewey, "Can We Let Jesus Die?," 138.

powers of his day. We know that such deaths also occur this way, as in the case of the 150,000 indigenous people who were killed or "disappeared" in Guatemala during the country's long civil war.

Whatever the historical details, the Scriptures proclaim that Jesus remained faithful to his call until the end. He accepted this cost and deliberately made his journey to Jerusalem. And he always trusted the God he called Father.

The mystery of suffering and death—Jesus's and others'—led the early Christian communities to search for light and meaning. They found in their knowledge of the culture, in the Hebrew Scriptures, and in their experience of Jesus's life and teachings a number of possibilities for interpretation. In a variety of ways they included these different interpretations in their stories and eventually in the Christian Scriptures.

Key Ideas of Tradition

The following generations of Christians, for almost two thousand years, have reflected on and developed these different interpretations, leading to theologies and popular pieties. Some of these have become well known and practiced extensively. Others, while orthodox, remain on the margins of many people's religious understanding and devotion.

In the early centuries of Christianity, we find much of this interpretation of Jesus's death continued. (See Michael Winter's *The Atonement* for a succinct summary.) Sacrifice and ransom were aspects of their world's culture, and atonement was already part of the tradition, though it was often simply presupposed by the patristic writers. Accordingly, as Winter notes, the patristic writers did not demonstrate about atonement the same "kind of profound philosophical investigation and elaboration which they brought to bear on the doctrines of the Trinity and the incarnation."[4]

There was, however, no unanimous teaching concerning how this reconciliation took place. Saint Ignatius of Antioch (ca. 110), for example, simply writes, "For he [Jesus] suffered all this on our account, that we might be saved."[5] And Saint Athanasius (ca. 350) writes, "So God sent his own son. . . . Now, all men had been condemned to death. But he who is innocent has offered for all his body to death."[6] Other writers stressed the incarnation as the cause of reuniting humanity with God (we will look more closely at these theologians, the Cappadocians, in the next chapter).

Tertullian (ca. 200) stressed legal concepts, a perspective later developed by Saint Augustine (ca. 400). The idea of satisfaction, in particular, had a significant impact on later theology, especially in the West. By using images of debts and justice, satisfaction meant that some form of compensation was necessary to right wrongs. So Augustine could write, "By his death, the one most real sacrifice offered for us, he [Jesus] purged, abolished, and extinguished whatever guilt there was which gave just ground for the principalities and powers to hold us in custody for our punishment."[7]

The legalistic approach received additional emphasis hundreds of years later by Saint Anselm (ca. 1100). His response to the question of why Jesus died on the cross, however, moved from justice and rights to honor and satisfaction. Reflecting the medieval culture of his day, Anselm understood sin to be something like a peasant insulting a king. Reconciliation would

---

4. Michael Winter, *The Atonement* (Collegeville, MN: Liturgical Press, 1995), 58.
5. Winter, *Atonement*, 41.
6. Winter, *Atonement*, 48.
7. Winter, *Atonement*, 57.

require satisfaction for this insult to the king's honor. Sin, however, is an infinite offense against God that demands adequate atonement. While humanity was obliged to atone, only God could do so adequately. That is exactly what Jesus, the God-man, accomplished by his acceptance of death. It was actually later theologians and preachers who added to Anselm's position by emphasizing blood and pain as the satisfaction that placated God's anger.[8]

An example of this view is found in the late Cardinal John O'Connor's address, "Who Will Care for the AIDS Victims?":

> We believe that it was not Christ's preaching or his teaching that made possible the salvation of the world nor was it his miracles, spectacular though they were. The salvation of the world became possible through Christ's suffering and death on the cross. Only when he was pinioned to the cross, helpless, burning with fever, parched with thirst, quivering with pain—only when he experienced the depth of loneliness and near-despair, with people spitting in his face and ridiculing him—only then was he saving the world. "If you are the Son of God," they shrieked at him, "prove it—save yourself, come down from the cross." He did not come down. Had he done so, his life would have been a failure.[9]

It is especially this later emphasis that is both widespread in today's church and yet problematic, as was described in chapter 1. So we turn now to an alternative interpretation, also expressed in Scripture and developed in tradition. This perspective views not only Jesus's death but also his life from a different angle, and so offers new light. At the same time, this view seems to be much closer to Jesus's own experience and vision.

---

8. Winter, *Atonement*, 63–65.
9. Cardinal John O'Connor, "Who Will Care for the AIDS Victims?" *Origins* 19, no. 33 (1990): 548.

For Reflection, Prayer, and Discussion

In this chapter we have considered the death of Jesus and several important images for interpreting it, including sacrifice and atonement.

1. What has the death of Jesus meant for your spiritual life? Do you remember any particular Good Friday services? What happened?

2. How do you understand and react to the themes of sacrifice and atonement? What Scripture passages are especially significant, positively or negatively?

3. What are your strongest reactions to the chapter's suggestions about the composition and meaning of the passion narrative?

4

The Word Made Flesh

"In the beginning was the Word. . . . And the Word became flesh and lived among us." (John 1:1, 14)

Most of us probably do not ask why God became flesh. If we did, our answers would likely sound something like this: "Jesus came to save us." Or more strongly: "Jesus came to die for our sins." Such convictions are found in the Scriptures and expressed in our liturgy, as we have already seen. The shadow of the cross falls on much of the tradition and popular piety.

There is, however, an alternative view about why God became human, expressed both in the Scriptures and in the Christian tradition. Though less well-known, this perspective that emphasizes God's overflowing love offers light for our understanding of Jesus, his suffering and death, and our own suffering. This chapter presents some of the key insights of the different perspective and suggests some implications for our everyday relationship with God. The next chapter will focus on Jesus's death and especially on our suffering.

The Cross

First, let's return to the shadow of the cross. Because the life, death, and resurrection of Jesus make up the foundation of Christianity, the Christian community has long reflected on their significance for our lives. What was the purpose of Jesus's life? Or simply, why Jesus?

The answer most frequently handed on in everyday religion, as we have seen in chapter 3, emphasizes sacrifice and atonement. This view returns to the creation story and sees in Adam and Eve's sin a fundamental alienation from God, a separation so profound that God must intervene to overcome it. The incarnation, the Word becoming flesh, is considered God's action to right this original wrong. The powerful images used to interpret Jesus's suffering and death colored the entire story, including the meaning of Jesus's birth and life. In many forms of theology, popular piety, and religious practice, the purpose of Jesus's life is directly linked to original sin and all human sinfulness. Without sin, there would have been no need for the incarnation.

Creation for Incarnation

An interpretation that highlights the incarnation stands beside this dominant view with its emphasis on sin. The alternate view is also expressed in Scripture (especially in John's Gospel and in Colossians and Ephesians) and has been developed through the centuries. Nevertheless, the emphasis on the Word made flesh has remained something of a "minority report," rarely gaining the same recognition and influence as the atonement view.

What, briefly, is the heart of this alternate interpretation? It holds that the whole purpose of creation is for the incarnation, God's sharing of life and love in a unique and definitive way. God becoming human is not an afterthought, an event to make up for original sin and human sinfulness. Incarnation is God's first thought, the original design for all creation. The purpose of Jesus's life is the fulfillment of the whole creative process, of God's eternal longing to become human.

For many of us who have lived a lifetime with the atonement view, it may be hard at first to hear the minority report. Yet it may offer some wonderful surprises for our relationship with God. From this perspective, God is appreciated with a different emphasis. God is not an angry or vindictive God, demanding the suffering and death of Jesus as a payment for past sin. God is, instead, a gracious God, sharing divine life and love in creation and in the incarnation (like parents sharing their love in the life of a new child). Such a view can dramatically change our image of God, our approach to suffering, and our day-by-day prayer.

In order to appreciate this emphasis more fully, let's take the time and effort to look at several of its most important expressions in Scripture and tradition. This brief review will also remind us that the focus on the incarnation is not just a new fad or some recent "feel good" theology. Its roots go back to the very beginning of Christianity. It may also be helpful to recall a statement from the *Catechism of the Catholic Church.* "Yet even if Revelation is already complete, it has not been made completely explicit; it remains for Christian faith gradually to grasp its full significance over the course of the centuries."[1] It is, then, our challenge and responsibility to consider seriously this minority view, searching to see how it might enlarge our appreciation and understanding of revelation.

He Pitched His Tent among Us

"In the beginning was the Word, and the Word was with God, and the Word was God. . . . All things came into being through him, and without him not one thing came into being. . . . And the Word became flesh." The prologue of John's Gospel (1:1–18) gives us this magnificent vision, proclaiming that all creation came to be in the Word, God's self-expression who became flesh, Jesus.

John's Gospel, written near the end of the first century, incorporated decades of preaching and reflection, of experiences of alienation from the Jewish community and acceptance in the gentile community, and of beginning dialogue with the philosophies of the age. The experience that began with personal encounter with Jesus of Nazareth leads to a vision reaching back to the beginning of time and offering a view of creation in and for Jesus. "He came to what was his own" (John 1:11).

John's meditation on God's supreme act of love in the incarnation (also see 3:16—"For God so loved the world that he gave his only Son, so that everyone who believes in him may not perish but may have eternal life") has led some theologians, as has been noted by Scripture scholar Raymond Brown, to consider that this event alone was sufficient to save the world. Indeed, John's Gospel does not see Jesus's death as a ransom (unlike the Synoptic Gospels, for example Mark 10:45), nor

---

1. John Paul II, *Catechism of the Catholic Church* (Liguori, MO: Liguori, 1994), #66.

does it use the language of sacrifice or atonement. There is instead emphasis on friendship, intimacy, mutuality, hospitality, service, and faithful love—revealing God's desire and gift for the full flourishing of humanity, or in other words, salvation (see the Farewell Address in John 13:1–17:26). Jesus's crucifixion (usually described as being "lifted up") is part of his "hour" of glorification, which also includes his resurrection and ascension. For John, this hour is not sacrifice but epiphany, the manifestation of God.

We may impose sacrificial imagery on John's Gospel because in our hearts and minds we blend together the four Gospels even though they give us very different portraits of Jesus. If we pay attention to John's emphasis on the incarnation and on the truth of God revealed in Jesus, we discover part of the foundation of our alternate answer to "Why Jesus?" For John, what is at the heart of reality is a God who wants to share divine life.

A Plan for the Fullness of Time

Another part of the foundation comes from Colossians and Ephesians. These two letters, written in the tradition of Paul in the latter part of the first century, also offer a cosmic vision. The letters look back to the beginning of time: "all things have been created through him [the beloved Son] and for him" (Col 1:16). And they look forward: God "has made known to us the mystery of his will, according to his good pleasure that he set forth in Christ, as a plan for the fullness of time, to gather up all things in him, things in heaven and things on earth" (Eph 1:9–10).

Especially these sections of the letters express remarkable beliefs: that Christ is the image of the invisible God, that God chose believers before the foundation of the world, that the goal of God's plan was the coming of Christ, that all things not only find their origin in Christ but are now held together in him and will be returned to right relationship with God through Christ, that God's overflowing grace has been lavished upon us.

Like John's prologue, Colossians and Ephesians connect with and express the Jewish wisdom tradition (see, for example, Proverbs 8; Wisdom 7 and 9). Wisdom was present with God from the beginning; everything was created in and through Wisdom. Unlike John's Gospel, Colossians and Ephesians include Paul's theology of the cross with their imagery of ransom and sacrifice. Many contemporary Scripture scholars judge that the author of Colossians added "making peace through the blood of his cross" (Col 1:20) to the already-existing hymn that makes up 1:15–20.

Ephesians and Colossians offer a magnificent vision of God's plan and initiative, revealed and fulfilled in Christ. This plan of salvation, an expression of God's wisdom, is eternal and not just an afterthought to sin. The letters acknowledge sin and sacrifice but emphasize God's overflowing love from before creation until the final fulfillment of the universe.

A Dance of Love

Throughout the centuries, the Christian community has carried on a dialogue with the Scriptures and the community's experience, always searching for understanding and appropriate ways to express its beliefs. Naturally, individual theologians and church councils made use of the philosophies and other insights of their age. Culture, politics, economics, and the questions of the day also influenced the expression of the church's faith.

During the first centuries of Christianity's existence, questions about Jesus and the Trinity raised special interest. How can we speak of this human being who is also God? How can we speak of one God who is Father, Son, and Spirit? (What many of us now simply accept as part of our creed had to be hammered out over many years.)

Three people who played a very important role in that process during the fourth century were Saint Basil of Caesarea, Saint Gregory of Nyssa, and Saint Gregory of Nazianzus. Because they lived in Cappadocia (an area of present-day Turkey), these three saints are simply called the Cappadocians. For many of us in the West, their thought is not well known.

A key concept in their thought about how the Trinity is both one and three is *perichoresis*, a term conveying dynamic and creative energy, eternal movement, mutuality, and interrelatedness. The three divine persons are what they are by relation to one another. Some scholars like to use the image of dance to describe this term. In this divine dance there is an eternal movement of reciprocal giving and receiving, expressing the essence and unity of God. Moreover, this interrelatedness of the triune God is not self-contained but poured out in creation, incarnation, and final fulfillment. God is overflowing love, leading humanity and all creation into the divine dance of God's life.

A Franciscan View

Hundreds of years later, in the Middle Ages, the question about Jesus was expressed very explicitly: Would the Son of God have become incarnate if humanity had not sinned? The great theologian Saint Thomas Aquinas (d. 1274), after acknowledging the different responses of theologians, answered in the negative. He viewed the incarnation as a remedy for sin. Thomas admitted, however, that God could have become incarnate even if sin had never occurred.

Another great philosopher-theologian, the Franciscan Blessed John Duns Scotus (d. 1308), disagreed with Thomas's emphasis on sin. Indeed, Duns Scotus boldly proclaimed and defended the primacy of the incarnation. He based his view on the Scriptures and early theologians and on logic. He argued, for example, that God's supreme work, the incarnation, had to be first and foremost in God's mind. It could not be dependent on or occasioned by any action of humans, especially sin.

Even more than logic, Duns Scotus emphasized divine love. God is love, the most perfect and orderly love. God created all life out of love in order to communicate to creatures the fullness of divine love. The incarnate Word is the foundation of the creative plan of God, the very reason for the existence of all creation, and the perfect expression of God's love. Following Colossians and Ephesians, Duns Scotus integrated redemption into this larger picture of love. The emphasis remains, however, on the primacy of Christ as the center and cornerstone of all creation.

The writings of Duns Scotus, with their careful reflection on the incarnation, supply the theoretical structure for the spirituality lived by Saint Francis of Assisi. This Christocentric emphasis has remained an essential dimension of Franciscan life and ministry.

Alpha and Omega

New and different questions emerged in the twentieth century. Jesuit scientist Pierre Teilhard de Chardin confronted the reality of evolution and realized the need for a new way to speak of the mystery of God. As a paleontologist, Teilhard studied fossils and other clues of our ancient past. As a believer, he returned to the foundations in Colossians and Ephesians and built on the long tradition that proclaimed Christ as the reason for the entire order of creation. He saw Christ as the Alpha (using an image from Rev 22:13), the very beginning of the evolutionary process, in whom all things were created (Col 1:15–16).

Teilhard especially looked to the future. From the scientific perspective, he saw that there had to be a point that governs the whole of evolution, a power of attraction that provides evolution's intrinsic drive and orientation. From the faith perspective, he saw that the glorified Christ is the Omega (using another image from Revelation), the final point in whom all things will be gathered up (Eph 1:10). Teilhard realized that the two perspectives focused on the same reality: Christ, the very soul of evolution, the Omega point in whom everything will be unified by and in love.

Teilhard struggled to heal the deep tension between science and religion that led so many to turn away from belief in God. He offered to the modern world an optimistic, cosmic, Christian humanism, uniting evolution and human efforts with the presence and action of Christ, all the while acknowledging the dark reality of evil. And so Teilhard could write in *How I Believe*,

> No, God does not hide himself to make us search for him, of that I am sure, much less to let us suffer in order to increase our merits. On the contrary, bent down over his creation which moves upwards to him, he works with all his power to give us happiness and light. Like a mother he watches over his newly born child. But our eyes are unable to see him yet. Is not precisely the whole course of centuries needed in order for our gaze to accustom itself to the light?[2]

2. Pierre Teilhard de Chardin, *How I Believe* (New York: Harper & Row, 1969), 89–90.

Though suspect for many years—what seemed radical in the 1920s became generally accepted in the 1960s—Teilhard's thought gradually exercised widespread influence, even on the Second Vatican Council. The Pastoral Constitution on the Church in the Modern World, for example, offers this vision in #45:

> The Word of God, through whom all things were made, was made flesh, so that as a perfect man he could save all women and men and sum up all things in himself. The Lord is the goal of human history, the focal point of the desires of history and civilization, the center of humanity, the joy of all hearts, and the fulfillment of all aspirations. . . . Animated and drawn together in his Spirit we press onwards on our journey towards the consummation of history which fully corresponds to the plan of his love: "to unite all things in him, things in heaven and things on earth" (Eph 1:10).[3]

God's Self-Communication

The twentieth century continued to raise serious questions and challenges to faith and religion. Numerous wars and other horrors led to pessimism and cynicism, doubt and denial. Relying on his extensive knowledge of the Christian tradition and of contemporary philosophies, Jesuit theologian Karl Rahner developed a profound response to these questions and challenges.

Rahner always stressed that God is holy and incomprehensible mystery. We have come to know the Trinitarian God (but never fully) in and through God's wonderful deeds in the world and in history. The very heart of this revelation, Rahner proclaimed, is God's self-communication: God's overflowing love

---

(This translation comes from Christopher Mooney's *Teilhard de Chardin and the Mystery of Christ* [New York: Image, 1968], 145.)

3. Austin Flannery, OP, ed., *Vatican Council II* (Northport, NY: Costello, 1996), 216.

leading to incarnation and so first to creation and grace and ultimately to beatific vision. In the rich tradition of John's Gospel and Ephesians, of the Cappadocians and Duns Scotus, Rahner wrote that God's free decision to communicate divine life and love can be viewed as the reason for creation and the world.

God's self-communication also occurs in the depths of our being. Rahner understood the human person as spirit in the world, a finite being with an infinite capacity. In every act of knowing and loving, we humans move toward God. We feel made for something more yet cannot reach our goal alone. If we are to satisfy our deepest human yearnings, we need grace. For Rahner, grace is God's self-gift, God's personal fulfillment of our natural openness offered freely to all persons, transforming the core of human life.

Like Teilhard, Rahner affirmed the presence of God in the whole world. All human experience offers the possibility of encounter with God. For Rahner, every day is "everyday," yet every hour is the hour of God's grace.

God's self-communication is not limited to individuals but extends to all creation. God's love is the real basis of the world's hope, both collective and cosmic. God's self-communication as the beatific vision will be the final fulfillment of all history and peoples. Then, indeed, God will be "all in all" (1 Cor 15:28).

Communion with the Living God

Another late-twentieth-century perspective was offered by Catherine Mowry LaCugna. In *God for Us* she creates from many of these earlier thoughts a striking and powerful interpretation, demonstrating her conviction that the "doctrine of the Trinity is ultimately a practical doctrine with radical consequences for Christian life."[4] For LaCugna, Trinitarian theology is not just an abstract treatment of God's inner life but is properly focused on God's life with humanity, especially as revealed in the events of salvation—through Jesus Christ in the Holy Spirit.

Accordingly, LaCugna incorporates much of Rahner's emphasis on salvation history as God's self-communication. Who and what God is, she affirms, "is fully expressed and bestowed in creation and history, particularly in the person of Jesus and the activity of the Spirit."[5]

She also uses and expands the Cappadocians' wonderful image of *perichoresis*. LaCugna locates this divine dance not just in God's inner life but in the mystery of the one communion of all persons, both divine and human. Borrowing themes of intimacy and communion from John's Gospel and Ephesians, she affirms that humanity has been made a partner in the divine dance "not through [humanity's] own merit but through God's election from all eternity. . . . The one *perichoresis*, the one mystery of communion includes God and humanity as beloved partners in the dance."[6] As a result, the equality, mutuality, and reciprocity expressed in Jesus's life and ministry give insight into God and into human relations.

These and numerous other carefully nuanced insights lead LaCugna to present a conclusion that speaks to every chapter in this book.

> The God who does not need nor care for the creature, or who is immune to our suffering, does not exist. The God too hidden for us to know, or too powerful to evoke anything but fear, does not exist. The God who watches us from a distance as an uninvolved, impartial observer, does not exist. The God conceived as a self-

4. Catherine Mowry LaCugna, *God for Us* (New York: HarperSanFrancisco, 1991), 1.
5. LaCugna, *God for Us*, 221.
6. LaCugna, *God for Us*, 274.

enclosed, exclusively self-related triad of persons does not exist. The God who keeps a ledger of our sins and failings, the divine policeman, does not exist. These are all false gods, fantasies of the imagination that has allowed itself to become detached from the rule of God's life disclosed in Jesus Christ. What we believe about God must match what is revealed of God in Scripture: God watches over the widow and the poor, God makes the rains fall on just and unjust alike, God welcomes the stranger and embraces the enemy.[7]

What Difference Does It Make?

For almost two thousand years, believers have found hope and light in recognizing the primacy of the incarnation. God's overflowing love wants to embody itself in and for others. Jesus is the first thought, not an afterthought. God creates in order to become flesh. Does this remarkable belief make any difference in our lives?

Absolutely, especially for those of us whose faith has been shaped by images of atonement and expiation. First, the creation-for-incarnation perspective highlights the rich meaning of Jesus. He is not plan B, sent simply to make up for sin. As Duns Scotus emphasized so well, God's masterpiece must result from something much greater and more positive (God's desire to share life and love). If some shadow of the cross remains in Christian tradition, it comes from the fact of Jesus's execution, a fact that does not express the full meaning and purpose of his life. There is more light than shadow: Jesus is the culmination of God's self-gift to the world.

Second, the focus on the Word made flesh helps us to appreciate the depth of our humanness and the importance of our actions. Rahner's marvelous musings on our life in a world of grace give us renewed understanding of the biblical phrase

7. LaCugna, *God for Us*, 397.

"created in God's image"—along with its many implications for how we treat all our sisters and brothers in the human family. His nuanced description of how God's saving will was fully realized in Jesus helps us to recognize both the cost of discipleship in our lives and the call to respond in faith, hope, and love to God's gracious love and forgiveness. Teilhard's cosmic vision inspires us to see and take our part in the great evolutionary process, in a particular way in our care for the earth.

Third and most important, our "minority report" offers us a new and transformed image of God. Many people have had an intuitive sense that the dominant perspective of God demanding the suffering and death of the Son as atonement has somehow missed the mark. Indeed, Rahner gently says that the idea of a sacrifice of blood offered to God may have been current at the time of Jesus, but it is of little help today. Rahner offers other interpretations of how Jesus saves us, emphasizing that God's saving will for all people was fully realized in Jesus through the response of his whole life.

Another contemporary scholar, Walter Wink, is more direct. He states that the early disciples simply were unable to sustain Jesus's vision of the compassionate and nonviolent reign of God. Overwhelmed by Jesus's horrible death and searching for some meaning, the disciples slipped back into an older religious conviction that believed violence (sacrifice) saves.

The emphasis on Jesus as the first thought can free us from those images and allows us to focus on God's overflowing love. This love is the very life of the Trinity and spills over into creation, grace, incarnation, and final flourishing and fulfillment. What a difference this makes for our relationship with God! We are invited into this divine dance. Life and love, not suffering and death, become the core of our spirituality and our morality. Our prayer—especially our celebration of the litur-

gical year—allows our spirits to soar in the light rather than
crouch in the shadow.

Another popular hymn ("I Danced in the Morning") captures
the spirit of this energizing view of life and love.

> I danced in the morning when the world was begun,
> And I danced in the moon and the stars and the sun,
> And I came down from heaven and I danced on the earth;
> At Bethlehem I had my birth. . . .
> I am the life that'll never, never die;
> I'll live in you if you'll live in me:
> I am the Lord of the dance, said he.
> Dance then wherever you may be;
> I am the Lord of the dance said he,
> And I'll lead you all, wherever you may be,
> And I'll lead you all in the dance, said he.[8]

"In the beginning was the Word . . . and the Word became
flesh." Alleluia!

For Reflection, Prayer, and Discussion

In this chapter we have considered the very different perspective of creation for the sake of incarnation.

1. What are your strongest reactions to this alternate
   view of the incarnation? How does it change your
   view of God?

2. Prayerfully read the Farewell Address in John's
   Gospel (13:1–17:26). Are there any sections that are
   especially important for you? Why?

3. What are the primary sources of darkness and of
   light in your life? In what ways does the alternate

---

8. Text by Sydney Carter.

view of incarnation transform your concerns and actions for a world of justice and peace?

5

Responding to the Mystery of Suffering

Emphasizing the God of life and love does not in any way deny the horror of the crucifixion. Jesus died a terrible death. The "minority view" offers, however, the possibility of different interpretations both of Jesus's death and our suffering. We don't have to believe in an angry God who demands Jesus's suffering and death as atonement. Scripture and tradition tell us of a God who is overflowing love, creates in order to become incarnate, and is forgiving, nonviolent, and compassionate. This God wants healing and salvation, not suffering—neither Jesus's nor our own.

Suffering and Salvation

The profound insights of contemporary theologians, especially Edward Schillebeeckx, OP, will help us develop and apply the positive implications of this alternative perspective. In his book, *What Are They Saying about the Theology of Suffering?*, Lucien Richard states, "To a greater extent than any other contemporary systematic theologian, Edward Schillebeeckx has developed his theology in confrontation with the universal situation of suffering."[1] Indeed, long sections of Schillebeeckx's *Christ* are devoted to suffering and salvation.

Schillebeeckx strongly affirms and holds together God's goodness with the reality of suffering, both in Jesus's life and in all human experience. A favorite expression of his goes like this: "God and suffering are diametrically opposed; where God appears, evil and suffering have to yield."[2] Because of God's overflowing love and compassion, God desires salvation for all people, including victory over their suffering. Schillebeeckx does not try to explain away the reality of suffering and evil in human history but sees them as rooted in finitude and freedom. Still he stresses that God's mercy is greater, as seen in Jesus's ministry and teaching. God does not want people to suffer but wills to overcome suffering wherever it occurs.

Human beings can benefit, Schillebeeckx acknowledges, from confronting suffering with courage and learning vulnerability and wisdom. Suffering for a righteous cause can also produce good. Nevertheless, he objects, there is too much suffering, "a barbarous excess."[3] Almost immediately he adds that such suffering is finally incomprehensible mystery; humans simply cannot explain or justify it. There is, however, a Christian response based on the story of Jesus.

> People do not *argue* against suffering, but tell a *story* and make statements on the basis of experience without giving an "expla-

---

1. Lucien Richard, OMI, *What Are They Saying about the Theology of Suffering?* (Mahwah, NJ: Paulist, 1992), 23.
2. Edward Schillebeeckx, *Christ* (New York: Seabury, 1980), 695.
3. Schillebeeckx, *Christ*, 725.

nation": simply because as Christians they look to the suffering and death of Jesus. It must have a meaning, even if no one knows how or why; the essential presupposition is that suffering should not be made light of. Faith in Jesus as Christ is an "answer" without arguments: a "nevertheless." Christianity does not give any explanation for suffering, but demonstrates a way of life. Suffering is destructively *real*, but it does not have the last word. Christianity seeks to hang on to both elements: no dualism, no dolorism, no theories about illusion—suffering is suffering and inhuman—however, there is more, namely God, as he shows himself in Jesus Christ.[4]

For Schillebeeckx, the center of Jesus's life was his relationship with God (as was developed in chap. 2 of this book). This intimacy with *Abba* was the foundation of Jesus's trust and hope, of his understanding of God as loving and compassionate. Such a God could not require the death of Jesus. Instead, Schillebeeckx sees Jesus's death as violent and negative. "*Negativity* cannot have a cause or a motive in God. But in that case we cannot look for a divine *reason* for the death of Jesus either. Therefore, first of all, we have to say that we are not redeemed *thanks* to the death of Jesus but *despite* it."[5]

Schillebeeckx joins many other contemporary scholars in emphasizing the link between Jesus's life and his death. Both Jesus's message and lifestyle challenged others, especially the powerful, and eventually led to his death. The meaning of Jesus's death cannot be separated from his life. When this happens—when theology and piety focus only on the death—then proper perspective is lost. Schillebeeckx strongly states, "Nor will the Christian blasphemously claim that God himself required the death of Jesus as compensation for what *we* make of our history. This sadistic mysticism of suffering is certainly

---

4. Schillebeeckx, *Christ*, 698–99.
5. Schillebeeckx, *Christ*, 729.

alien to the most authentic tendencies of the great Christian tradition, at the very least."[6]

What is redemptive is not the negativity of suffering and death but the positivity of love, a love expressed concretely in Jesus's healing, teaching, and trusting and confirmed in the resurrection. Redemptive love, for Schillebeeckx, changes the world, forgives, and reconciles. And so he claims that we catch a glimpse of salvation when we encounter others in love. "But salvation, wholeness, is possible only in perfection and universality,"[7] which, of course, can be promised to us only through the love of God.

It is the resurrection of Jesus, specifically, that shows God's determination to overcome the negative and destructive aspects of history. We can trust that neither suffering nor death can separate us from God. Of course, as Schillebeeckx notes, our faith in the resurrection is vulnerable and not visibly justified by the facts of history. "The servant is not greater than his Lord. Just as Jesus did, the Christian takes the risk of entrusting himself and the vindication of his living to God; he is prepared to receive the vindication where Jesus did: beyond death."[8]

This trust and freedom also allow and energize the Christian to overcome suffering and to work for more wholeness (justice, happiness, authentic flourishing) now. Especially in his later work, Schillebeeckx emphasized the imperative of social action, that is, political protest and transformation of the social structures responsible for oppression and injustice. He high-

6. Schillebeeckx, *Christ*, 728.
7. Schillebeeckx, *Christ*, 834.
8. Schillebeeckx, *Jesus*, 643.

lighted our solidarity with the outcasts of the world, the solidarity that makes us God's partners in salvation.[9]

Schillebeeckx shares this emphasis especially with liberation theologians. Writing in the general context of poverty and oppression in El Salvador and in the specific context of the 2001 earthquake, Jesuit Jon Sobrino also addresses the ancient question of God and suffering (theodicy). He notes that some people (he calls them extremists) claimed that the earthquake was God's punishment for sin. He adds that an archbishop in Guatemala made a similar judgment after the earthquake there in 1976. Sobrino responds, however, calling this type of message "an insult to God" that is also "unjustly harmful to human beings" because it intensifies their spiritual anguish.[10]

Another reaction to the earthquake was simply submission, "God's will be done." Sobrino sees this response as understandable in El Salvador's traditional religious culture but finally not satisfying, especially in the even more difficult times of civil war. Then the question was a profound, "What's wrong with God?"

Sobrino offers his own response, one that recognizes the mystery of God and suffering.[11] "Our only choice, I believe, is to live with a theodicy unresolved in theory, and with a practice that goes on opening a pathway—with God walking it beside us—through the history of suffering."[12] Later he describes the theological foundation for this view while pondering the crucified God and the meaning of redemption: "It is the love of Jesus (and of God) that saves, not bloodshed. The love of Jesus saves

---

9. Kathleen McManus, OP, "Suffering in the Theology of Edward Schillebeeckx," *Theological Studies* 60, no. 3 (1999): 487.

10. Jon Sobrino, *Where Is God? Earthquake, Terrorism, Barbarity, and Hope* (Maryknoll, NY: Orbis, 2004), 138.

11. Sobrino, *Where Is God?*, 139–40.

12. Sobrino, *Where Is God?*, 142.

human beings, especially victims; love that stays through to the end, even if it leads to a cross. That is what we call redemption. I think everyone can understand that, with no need for a sacrificial interpretation."[13]

How then, in summary, do the thoughts of Schillebeeckx and Sobrino help us to appreciate more fully the "minority report" found in Scripture and tradition? First, their insistence on the utter goodness of God, who does not want us to suffer, encourages us to let go of the negative and even threatening images of God handed on in some interpretations and pieties. We turn instead to the God of overflowing love; we join in the divine dance.

Second, from this perspective we contemplate the suffering and death of Jesus. We understand how such a God could not require Jesus's death for our salvation. Instead, *Abba* God must have, to use human terms, suffered. How could it be otherwise for the God of life and love, the covenanted partner, the tender and gracious parent?

Third, we expand our view of salvation, then, to include all of Jesus's life, including his teaching, healing, and his very person. Rooted in his experience of God as *Abba*, Jesus revealed God's desire for our well-being, wholeness, and fulfillment—in friendship, intimacy, mutuality, service, and faithful love. Jesus's own deep and abiding trust in God is confirmed in the resurrection.

Fourth, rooted in resurrection hope, we are freed to engage the powers of oppression and injustice in our world and join in God's work of overcoming suffering. This suffering, of course, includes all that confronts us personally and directly. We must now consider in more detail our response to this suffering.

---

13. Sobrino, *Where Is God?*, 148.

Responding to Suffering

The emphasis on God's overflowing love, as expressed in Scripture and tradition and developed by Schillebeeckx, Sobrino, and other contemporary authors, moves beyond our natural question of "Why?" and suggests four elements of a response to suffering: acknowledge the suffering, trust in God, act, and stand in awe.

Articulate the Agony

The first step in responding to suffering is simply being truthful, avoiding denial (which can be so easy), and admitting the pain and horror of the suffering, whatever the cause. We must never glorify suffering. Yes, it can lead us to deeper maturity and wisdom, but suffering can also crush the human spirit.

In *Engaging the Powers*, Walter Wink offers a haunting image to assist us in naming our suffering. He writes,

> We are so interconnected with all of life that we cannot help being touched by the pain of all that suffers. . . . We are literally inundated with news of suffering from all round the globe, and it cannot but affect us. . . . We human beings are far too frail and tiny to bear all this pain. The solution is not avoidance, however. Refusal to read the papers or listen to the news is no protection. I am convinced that our solidarity with all of life is somatic, and that we sense the universal suffering whether we wish to or not. What we need is a portable form of the Wailing Wall in Jerusalem, where we can unburden ourselves of this accumulated suffering. We need to experience it; it is a part of reality. . . . We are to articulate these agonizing longings and let them pass through us to God. Only the heart at the center of the universe can endure such a weight of suffering.[14]

14. Walter Wink, *Engaging the Powers* (Minneapolis: Fortress Press, 1992), 305.

This same insight was expressed long before Wink—by the psalmist. We have already heard a few samples of the lament psalms in chapter 1. These psalms—and there are many of them, including 3, 5, 17, 22, 25, 39, 44, 53, 77, 88, 89, 109, 143—follow a standard pattern. The psalm begins with an invocation of God and a cry for help. Sometimes an expression of trust also forms part of an extended introduction. The description of the suffering (whether sickness or death or persecution) and a request for help (sometimes even including an imperative addressed to God) make up the heart of the psalm. The language may be striking, even stereotypical of lament. The conclusion, however, often introduces a different tone, one of trust and certainty.

Let's listen to Psalm 17 as an example.

Hear a just cause, O Lord; attend to my cry;
give ear to my prayer from lips free of deceit.
From you let my vindication come;
let your eyes see the right. . . .
Guard me as the apple of the eye;
hide me in the shadow of your wings,
from the wicked who despoil me,
my deadly enemies who surround me.
They close their hearts to pity;
with their mouths they speak arrogantly.
They track me down;
now they surround me;
they set their eyes to cast me to the ground.
They are like a lion eager to tear,
like a young lion lurking in ambush.
Rise up, O Lord, confront them, overthrow them!
By your sword deliver my life from the wicked,
from mortals—by your hand, O Lord—from mortals
whose portion in life is in this world.
May their bellies be filled with what you have stored up for them;
may their children have more than enough;
may they leave something over to their little ones.

As for me, I shall behold your face in righteousness;
when I awake I shall be satisfied,
beholding your likeness. (Ps 17:1–2, 8–15)

Lament marked the very beginning of the history of the Hebrew people—and so the beginning of our religious story, too. In their oppression, the people cried out to God, and God heard and acted, leading them to freedom. "After a long time the king of Egypt died. The Israelites groaned under their slavery, and cried out. Out of the slavery their cry for help rose up to God. God heard their groaning, and God remembered his covenant with Abraham, Isaac, and Jacob. God looked upon the Israelites, and God took notice of them" (Exod 2:23–25).

Lament is necessary for individuals. Things are not right in our lives: sickness, poverty, abuse, alienation, drugs, violence, death. The first step to grief and healing is to move from overwhelmed silence to the bold speech of lament. The psalms show us how to speak out against suffering and oppression, even against God. But such crying out allows us both to grieve and to grow into a mature covenant partner with God and not merely a subservient one.

Lament is also necessary for life in society, raising questions of justice and power. Another Scripture scholar, Walter Brueggemann, writes strongly in his "The Costly Loss of Lament,"

> For the managers of the system—political, economic, religious, moral—there is always a hope that the troubled folks will not notice the dysfunction or that a tolerance of a certain degree of dysfunction can be accepted as normal and necessary, even if unpleasant. Lament occurs when the dysfunction reaches an unacceptable level, when the injustice is intolerable and change is insisted upon.[15]

15. Walter Brueggemann, "The Costly Loss of Lament," *Journal for the Study of the Old Testament* 36 (1986): 62.

Trust in God

Lament allows us to move from silence to speech. It renews and deepens our relationship with God, even as it challenges God. And so it leads naturally to the second element in our response to suffering: trust in God.

Trusting in God, of course, is especially challenging in the dark times of suffering. One usual response is initially just the opposite. We question how God could cause this suffering or at least allow it. We ask why. We may complain to God or even begin to doubt God's existence. That is exactly why the lament psalms can be so helpful, matching our experience and emotions. The lament also allows us to stay in conversation with God, deepening the relationship and gradually moving to a new trust.

Job also stands as an example of this process. The extensive suffering tests Job's faithfulness. Job challenges the dominant theology that judges him to be sinful, and he cries out for a hearing with God. After listening to God's response, Job moves from boldness to nuanced appreciation of the mystery of life and to humble but renewed friendship with God, a God who was with Job throughout the ordeal even though Job was unaware.

An even greater example of trust in God, of course, is Jesus. We have already considered in chapter 2 Jesus's relationship with *Abba* and how this love shaped Jesus's life, vision, and ministry. The gospels are quite clear in describing trust as the center of Jesus's life.

Jesus directly addressed the topic of trust. "Therefore I tell you, do not worry about your life, what you will eat, or about your body, what you will wear. . . . Consider the lilies, how they grow: they neither toil nor spin. . . . Instead strive for his [God's] kingdom, and these things will be given to you as well" (Luke 12:22–31). Similarly, "Are not two sparrows sold for a penny? Yet not one of them will fall to the ground apart from your Father. And even the hairs of your head are all counted. So do not be afraid; you are of more value than many sparrows" (Matt 10:29–31). And again:

> Ask, and it will be given you; search, and you will find; knock, and the door will be opened for you. For everyone who asks receives, and everyone who searches finds, and for everyone who knocks, the door will be opened. Is there anyone among you who, if your child asks for bread, will give a stone? Or if the child asks for a fish, will give a snake? If you then, who are evil, know how to give good gifts to your children, how much more will your Father in heaven give good things to those who ask him! (Matt 7:7–11)

Surely, trust in God also provided the basis for many other teachings, for example, the Beatitudes. "Blessed are you who are poor, for yours is the kingdom of God. Blessed are you who are hungry now, for you will be filled. Blessed are you who weep now, for you will laugh" (Luke 6:20–21). Whether this trust allowed Jesus to face likely threats or whether the trust was so complete that Jesus was simply unconcerned about his fate, trust in God fueled his words and actions, including his final journey to Jerusalem. The resurrection can rightly be considered God's confirmation of Jesus's trust.

Two contemporary followers of Jesus offer us some reflections that embody the trust of Job and Jesus. Oscar Romero, archbishop of San Salvador, faced massive suffering during El Salvador's civil war. Thousands of his people, including sisters, priests, and catechists, were being tortured and killed. As Romero spoke out more and more boldly against oppression and injustice, his own life was threatened. Indeed, he would die a martyr's death while celebrating the Eucharist. Before his death, Romero spoke about the paradox of suffering and faith. "God exists, and he exists even more, the farther you feel from him. God is closer to you when you think he is farther away and doesn't hear you. When you feel the anguished desire for God to come near because you don't feel him present, then God is very close to your anguish."[16]

Cardinal Joseph Bernardin died in very different circumstances. The archbishop of Chicago was very open about his cancer, first his attempts to seek healing and then his decision to stop treatment. His suffering and death touched the hearts of millions of people. Before his death, Bernardin simply yet powerfully presented some of his reflections in *The Gift of Peace*. He moved away from older interpretations of suffering and instead emphasized compassionate solidarity. For Bernardin, suffering in communion with Jesus made all the difference. "Perhaps, the ultimate burden is death itself. It is often preceded by pain and suffering, sometimes extreme hardships. . . . But notice that Jesus did not promise to take away our burdens. He promised to help us carry them. And if we let go of ourselves—and our own resources—and allow the Lord to help us, we will be able to see death not as an enemy or a threat but as a friend."[17]

Trust in God, of course, is a gift of grace. Still, are there ways to nourish our response to this gift? What inspired the psalmist, Job, Romero, Bernardin, Jesus, and so many others not mentioned here—for example, Ruth and Jeremiah, Mary and Joseph, and the many other modern martyrs? One key inspiration must have been remembering and celebrating God's saving deeds. For us Christians today, gathering to tell

---

16. Archbishop Oscar Romero, *The Violence of Love* (San Francisco: Harper & Row, 1988), 158.
17. Cardinal Joseph Bernardin, *The Gift of Peace* (Chicago: Loyola Press, 1977), 126.

the story of Jesus and to be nourished with his body and blood is the privileged event for deepening our trust in God. Our eucharistic celebration leads us into the divine dance, offering us light especially for dark times and inviting us to be light for others. Surely it does not stop suffering but does bring us together as a faithful community and then sends us out as a compassionate people. And so we need prayerful liturgies and vibrant parishes. We can accept the cost of discipleship because we follow Jesus in trusting God.

Act

This trust both allows and inspires our action, the third element in our response to suffering. Following the life and ministry of Jesus, we work as individuals and as communities to overcome and end suffering. Our actions move in three directions: toward other individuals, toward the political and economic structure of society, and toward ourselves.

Suffering evokes our compassion. We have already considered several examples of such compassion in the Scriptures, including Jesus's healing of the leper. We recognize that we may not be able to heal, despite modern medicine's remarkable achievements. Still, we can embody God's love by remaining with others in their suffering. Job's friends initially did this so well: they came and sat in silent grief with him.

Along with companionship, concrete and direct compassion can take other forms also. Preparing meals, running errands, providing transportation, and praying with people are real ways to assist others and to suffer with them (the very meaning of *compassion*).

Our reflections on lament earlier in this chapter raised awareness of the social origins of suffering. As Brueggemann pointed out, lament occurs when injustice becomes intolerable and change is demanded. He adds that when lament is not allowed, justice questions gradually become ignored. When this happens, we miss the public, systemic issues about which "biblical faith is relentlessly concerned."[18] The Hebrew people cried out to God, complaining about their oppression. God heard them and did something: God freed them and led them to the promised land. Humanity, of course, has always been called to join in God's saving deeds. So we are now called to hear the laments of our sisters and brothers in today's world—and to act.

Awareness of the world's suffering can certainly feel overwhelming. As Wink reminds us, however "frail and tiny" we may be, it is important not to avoid the pain. Instead, we must lament and pray and act, integrating contemplation and action. "Social action without prayer is soulless; but prayer without action lacks integrity."[19]

The needs are so great and the systemic issues so complex: globalization, massive economic injustice and oppression, unbelievable violence. What can one person do? Wink offers sound guidance, urging us "to seek the specific shape of our own divine calling in the day-to-day working out of our relationship with God."[20] He explains, "We are not called to do everything, to heal everything, to change everything, but only to do what God asks of us. And in the asking is supplied the power to perform it. We are freed from the paralysis that results from being overwhelmed by the immensity of the need and our relative powerlessness, and we are freed from mes-

18. Brueggemann, "Loss of Lament," 64.
19. Wink, *Engaging the Powers*, 306.
20. Wink, *Engaging the Powers*, 307.

sianic megalomania, in which we try to heal everyone that hurts."[21]

Our action searches in solidarity with others for creative and courageous ways to overcome suffering and its causes in our world. While we cannot do everything, we can at least do one thing: for example, support Bread for the World, tutor in inner-city schools, learn about nonviolent conflict transformation, and organize parish study groups concerning the many systemic threats to life.

We recognize that some of these actions may even lead to suffering in our own lives. Fidelity to the life of discipleship—embodying a consistent ethic of life in our ordinary choices about relationships, work, and politics—can be costly. So, our third direction of action is toward ourselves, as disciples and as sufferers.

In this context of confronting sinful social structures, the witness of Archbishop Romero and so many other martyrs speaks powerfully about the cost of discipleship. For them, the cost was indeed dramatic: intense oppression and finally violent death. For most of us, the cost is very ordinary, coming in our everyday efforts to confront consumerism, individualism, violence, and many other forms of evil.

In our families and communities and in our hearts, we experience the tension generated by living in a consumer society flooded with advertising. This market gospel values things rather than people, profits rather than human dignity and rights. Looking out for "number one" replaces concern for the common good as the center of political and economic life. Media of all kinds glorify violence as a response to difficult situations. Government policies and actions reinforce a culture

---

21. Wink, *Engaging the Powers*, 307.

of death. Oppressive social and religious systems limit efforts to live Jesus's vision of inclusivity, compassion, and love. And always the dark mystery of evil challenges belief in a good and gracious God.

Faithful witness can be very costly, even when embedded in these everyday realities of personal relationships and social structures. So we need to act to deepen our commitment as disciples. Jesus and the martyrs have clearly offered us the way: radical trust in a compassionate and present God, forgiveness, bold actions that break down barriers and old alienations, solidarity and tender love, and, yes, the willingness to accept the implications of faithfulness to God's call.

Of course, we also suffer from sickness and the many other personal ills already discussed in this book. How are we to act in these situations? We may need to lean against some of the imperatives we have learned from our culture, such as individualism and self-sufficiency. In our suffering we will need to reach out to others, ask for their help, receive what they offer, and allow them to accompany us in the deep abyss.

As we reach out to humans, so too we move toward God (who may seem very distant) in lament, praise, or gratitude. Perhaps some of the great stories in the Scriptures describing God's overflowing love and desire for healing and wholeness can encourage and comfort us—even in the darkness—and renew our search for God.

Stand in Awe

These actions bring us to the fourth element of the response to suffering: we stand in awe of suffering and of God. We know that it is a human reaction to ask why, to search for meaning and reasons for our suffering. We have seen, however, that such efforts often have led to unsatisfying and even problematic perspectives. Suffering remains a mystery, not a problem to be solved. We stand with Job at the end of his bold contest with God: "See, I am of small account; what shall I answer you? I lay my hand on my mouth. I have spoken once, and I will not answer; twice, but will proceed no further. . . . Therefore I have uttered what I did not understand, things too wonderful for me, which I did not know" (Job 40:4–5; 42:3).

The "minority report," rooted in Scripture and tradition and developed in this book, gives us even more, offering an approach to suffering that stresses God's overflowing love. God does not desire suffering but works to overcome it. God did not demand Jesus's suffering and does not want ours. From the beginning, God is a God of life and love, creating all to be part of the divine dance, sharing life with us in a unique and definitive way in Jesus. In the context of trusting this gentle God, we are to lament and act to overcome suffering even as we acknowledge its incomprehensibility and marvel at God's remarkable respect of human freedom. We know that some suffering results from our own and other persons' evil choices (injustice and terrorism, for example). We know that other suffering simply happens in a world that is not yet fulfilled (earthquakes, debilitating diseases, etc.). Finally, however, suffering is not fully understandable. The approach we have explored in this book allows us to move past "Why?" and ask instead, "How can I respond? What can we do now?" A profound trust in a gracious God allows us to ask these questions and then to act. This trust allows us, finally, to stand in awe of the mystery of suffering and the mystery of God's faithful love.

A Fundamental Change

The traditional emphasis on suffering as sacrifice and atonement seems initially to offer more reason and therefore comfort in our suffering. We seem to endure suffering better if there is a cause or some meaning. This, of course, is true even as we look back at Jesus's horrible suffering. We may be consoled to think that Jesus suffered and died for our sins.

As we have seen in this book, however, this comfort comes at much too high a price—an image of God that finally is unacceptable; a God who threatens, tests, or tortures is simply not the God revealed by Jesus. We must test every interpretation of and every perspective on suffering by asking, What does this say about God? Letting go of the traditional view of suffering with its implications of sacrifice and atonement may feel like a great loss. Ultimately, however, there will be a great gain: encountering the God of love and life and participating in the divine dance. It may take time and effort to let go of the atonement perspective, but translating familiar Scripture passages and liturgical texts in terms of this divine dance will produce surprising peace and hope.

A Meditation

Suffering remains both horror and mystery, and so invites prayer. Here is an image for meditation.

Recall Michelangelo's magnificent sculpture, *Pietà*. The grieving mother of Jesus holds his dead body in her arms. Feel the pain, the sorrow, the horror. Then allow the sculpture to become a symbol, to take on other meanings. First, perhaps, the symbol of the world's mothers holding their battered sons and daughters, victims of wars and other violence. Then let the sculpture speak of a gentle God holding God's torn and bloodied world. Finally, let it be God holding your broken spirit.

Our God suffers with us. In the depths of suffering, we too may cry out, "My God, my God, why have you forsaken me?" In the darkness, we need to express our lament but finally our trust that the gracious, compassionate God does hold our broken bodies and spirits.

We can trust because there is more: our God is a God of resurrection, of new life. The story did not end with the cross, with suffering and death. No, God raised Jesus to new and transformed life. And we are an Easter people. That truth, ultimately, is at the very heart of our response to suffering. God suffers with us, leads us as individuals and as communities in resisting evil, and brings us all to the fullness of life.

For Reflection, Prayer, and Discussion

In this chapter we have considered the rich thought of Edward Schillebeeckx and others on suffering and then four specific aspects of our response to suffering.

1. Was one of the ideas in this chapter especially important or troubling for you? What implications does it have for your day-to-day living?

2. What in your life now calls for lament? Prayerfully read the suggested psalms and find those that fit your experience. What is your response to Wink's statement, "Social action without prayer is soulless; but prayer without action lacks integrity"?

3. How do you experience and express trust in God, which is rooted in the resurrection and transforms all life—including suffering?

6

The Mystery of God

In the introduction we met the woman struggling with the traditional theology of a God who demands Jesus's suffering and death. Our conversation that evening briefly covered a number of the key ideas of this book. What a great and wonderful relief these ideas offered the woman, who responded with tears of joy and freedom!

She—and most of us—will continue, of course, to shed tears of sorrow as we confront suffering and death. A different theological perspective, as we have seen, not only suggests other interpretations of Jesus's suffering but also gives us alternative ways to respond to our own pain. We entrust all of our lives to our gentle and loving God.

The mystery of suffering has led us into the mystery of God. God, the Alpha and Omega, the beginning and end of all life, is the center of the believer's life. But how can we speak of

God?[1] What images do we find helpful in trying to describe that which cannot be fully described?

The images we have of God play an important role in how our relationship with God, the heart of our spiritual-moral life, develops. If, as we grew up, we were taught about a God who judges and punishes us, then our relationship might be characterized by fear or even avoidance. If, instead, God's love and forgiveness had been emphasized, we probably would have a very different relationship with God, one characterized by warmth and acceptance.

The Eucharist and other sacraments, in addition to private prayer, continue to influence our images of God and shape our relationship. Other experiences, past and present, also influence how we think and feel about God, for example, if we had an abusive father or if we have experienced a deep and unconditional love. As we have seen, suffering frequently raises profound questions about God: "Why did God do this?" or even "Is there a God?"

A wise Scripture scholar once said that we need to *multiply* our images of God.[2] Different images help us to appreciate different aspects of God, who is always greater than any one description. But each image can give us a glimpse of the Holy One, the source and goal of all life, and so nurture our relationship with God.

The Bible itself offers us a wonderful variety of images of God, including fire, shepherd, warrior, shelter, light, bread of life, love, and Holy One. Two that we may take for granted are woman and man: God created humans in God's image; in the

---

1. See Michael J. Buckley, SJ, "Within the Holy Mystery," in *A World of Grace*, ed. Leo O'Donovan, SJ (Washington, DC: Georgetown University Press, 1995), 31–49.
2. Barbara E. Bowe, RSCJ, *Biblical Foundations of Spirituality* (Lanham, MD: Rowman & Littlefield, 2017).

divine image God created them; male and female God created them (see Gen 1:27). Human beings are icons of God.

One perhaps surprising image is God as rock! Listen to the psalmist: "I love you, O Lord, my strength. The Lord is my rock, my fortress, and my deliverer, my God, my rock in whom I take refuge" (Ps 18:1–2). "[God] alone is my rock and my salvation, my fortress; I shall never be shaken" (Ps 62:2). Hardly an image of tenderness or compassion! Yet the psalmist is comfortable calling God a rock. The prophet Isaiah also says, "Trust in the Lord forever, for in the Lord God you have an everlasting rock" (Isa 26:4).

Other passages in the Bible speak of God in maternal terms. "You forgot the God who gave you birth" (Deut 32:18b). Similarly, the unknown prophet known as Second Isaiah with the people in exile had God ask, "Can a woman forget her nursing child, or show no compassion for the child of her womb? Even these may forget, yet I will never forget you" (Isa 49:15). In the Wisdom literature especially (see Wis 7:7–8:8, for example) and throughout the Bible, there are many feminine references and images, some based on biological activity (like giving birth) and others on women's cultural activities (like being a midwife).

The prophet Hosea describes God as a gentle parent. "When Israel was a child I loved him, and out of Egypt I called my son. The more I called them, the more they went from me. . . . Yet it was I who taught Ephraim to walk, I took them up in my arms; . . . I led them with cords of human kindness, with bands of love" (Hos 11:1–4).

Jesus calls God *Abba* (Daddy), and two of his parables pair feminine and masculine images of God: a woman looking for a lost coin and a father looking for a lost son (see Luke 15). These and other parables and teachings point to an intimate, loving relationship with a merciful and faithful God.

All these biblical images of God may help us appreciate characteristics of God like gentle compassion, faithfulness, strength, and love. Still, along with the images must come some caution. "If we use words hewn from the things around us for God, we reduce Him to a thing around us."[3] God is always more, always other. God is neither male nor female, neither shepherd nor rock!

In many of his writings, theologian Karl Rahner, SJ, offers a different kind of image and so helps us to think carefully about the reality behind all images. He never ceases to remind us that God is more than we can ever explain or articulate. God is Holy Mystery, the Incomprehensible One, the Loving Abyss.

In the chapter on Rahner in her *Quest for the Living God*, Elizabeth Johnson concisely presents the heart of Rahner's insight. "This one holy mystery is the ineffable God who while remaining eternally a plentitude—infinite, incomprehensible, inexpressible—wishes to self-communicate to the world, and does so in the historically tangible person of Jesus Christ and in the grace of the Spirit so as to become the blessedness of every person and of the universe itself."[4]

Johnson spells out this remarkable sentence emphasizing two parts: God's transcendence and God's immanence. Transcendence speaks of God's otherness, always greater and more, not a particular being (like you and I and all other creatures) but the ground of being (Unlimited Being). Because God is transcendent, God can be immanent, meaning intimate nearness, within all that is.

---

3. Buckley, "Within the Holy Mystery," 41.
4. Elizabeth Johnson, *Quest for the Living God* (New York: Continuum, 2007), 43.

God's self-communication has taken place in Jesus, "the human person in whom God's irrevocable union with humanity in self-giving love is decisively achieved and revealed."[5] God's self-communication also takes place in God's Spirit given directly to all human beings—what we call grace.

Despite his emphasis on God as mystery, Rahner still uses aspects of our physical world to point us in the right direction. Those who live near an ocean (or have visited one) experience the endless immensity of the water when looking out toward the horizon. Rahner comments that we humans are "forever occupied with the grains of sand along the shore" where we dwell "at the edge of the infinite ocean of mystery."[6] Sitting at the edge of the Grand Canyon and peering into the depths can also help make real the meaning of an abyss.

Rahner's emphasis on Holy Mystery may be especially helpful in times of doubt, darkness, and suffering. In the distant past the psalmist described suffering as a dark abyss (Psalm 88); Rahner describes God as a loving abyss, an abyss deserving our awe, wonder, and worship. He speaks of Jesus's experience of the abyss:

> There is Jesus, a human being who loves, who is faithful unto death, in whom all of human existence, life, speech and action, is open to the mystery which he calls his Father and to which he surrenders in confidence even when all is lost. For him the immeasurable dark abyss of his life is the Father's protecting hand. And so he holds fast to love for human beings and also to his one hope even when everything seems to be being destroyed in death, when it no longer seems possible to love God and human beings.[7]

5. Otto Hentz, SJ, "Anticipating Jesus Christ: An Account of Our Hope," in *A World of Grace*, 113.
6. Karl Rahner, SJ, "The Experience of God Today," in *Theological Investigations XI* (New York: Seabury, 1974), 159.
7. Karl Rahner, SJ, "Why Am I a Christian Today?," in *The Practice of Faith* (New York: Crossroad, 1986), 8.

Rahner also turns to his own experience:

> What could I put in the place of Christianity? Only emptiness, despair, night, and death. And what reason do I have to consider this abyss as truer and more real than the abyss of God? It is easier to let oneself fall into one's own emptiness than into the abyss of the Blessed Mystery. But it is not more courageous or truer. This truth, of course, shines out only when it is also loved and accepted since it is the truth which makes us free and whose light consequently begins to shine only in the freedom which dares all to the very height.... [This truth] gives me the courage to believe in it and to call to it when all the dark despairs and lifeless voids would swallow me up.[8]

Multiplying our images of God can enrich and enliven our relationship with God. The image beyond other images—God as Holy Mystery, Loving Abyss—captures the wonder of God and offers hope and light in times of doubt and darkness, of suffering and death. Like sitting at the edge of the Grand Canyon, we look into the abyss of mystery: first, mystery that is suffering, but ultimately so much more, the holy mystery who is God. In suffering and finally in death, we express our deep and abiding trust and hope:

> May songs of the angels welcome you,
> and guide you along your way.
> May the smiles of the martyrs greet your own
> as darkness turns into day.
> Ev'ry fear will be undone,
> and death will be no more,
> as songs of the angels bring you home
> before the face of God.
> From the depths I cry to You, O Lord.
> Hear the sound of my pleading.
> For my soul longs for You, O Lord,
> like the watchman longs for day.

8. Karl Rahner, SJ, "Thoughts on the Possibility of Belief Today," in *Theological Investigations V* (Baltimore: Helicon, 1966), 8–9.

I know that my Redeemer lives;
and He shall stand,
shall stand upon the earth.
And I shall see, and I shall see.
Behold! I tell you a myst'ry:
we shall all be changed.
For the trumpet shall sound, the dead be raised
in the victory, the glory of our God.
May songs of the angels welcome you,
and guide you along your way.
May the smiles of the martyrs greet your own
as darkness turns into day.
Ev'ry fear will be undone,
and death will be no more,
as songs of the angels bring you home
before the face of God.[9]

9. Bob Dufford, SJ, "Songs of the Angels," in *The Steadfast Love*, ed. St. Louis Jesuits (Phoenix: North American Liturgy Resources, 1985).

Selected Bibliography

Armstrong, Karen, and Fellows of the Jesus Seminar. *The Once and Future Faith*. Santa Rosa, CA: Polebridge, 2001.

Bernardin, Cardinal Joseph. *The Gift of Peace*. Chicago: Loyola Press, 1997.

Billman, Kathleen, and Daniel Migliore. *Rachel's Cry*. Cleveland: United Church Press, 1999.

Bonansea, B. M., OFM. *Man and His Approach to God in John Duns Scotus*. Lanham, MD: University Press of America, 1983.

Bowe, Barbara E., RSCJ. *Biblical Foundations of Spirituality*. 2nd ed. Lanham, MD: Rowman & Littlefield, 2017.

Brown, Raymond, SS. *An Adult Christ at Christmas*. Collegeville, MN: Liturgical Press, 1978.

———. *The Birth of the Messiah*. New York: Doubleday, 1977.

———. *A Crucified Christ in Holy Week*. Collegeville, MN: Liturgical Press, 1986.

———. *The Death of the Messiah*. New York: Doubleday, 1994.

———. *Reading the Gospels with the Church*. Cincinnati: St. Anthony Messenger, 1996.

Brueggemann, Walter. "The Costly Loss of Lament." *Journal for the Study of the Old Testament* 36 (1986): 57–71.

Dewey, Arthur J., Roy W. Hoover, Lane C. McGaughy, and Daryl D. Schmidt. *The Authentic Letters of Paul*. Salem, OR: Polebridge, 2010.

Dewey, Arthur J. *Inventing the Passion: How the Death of Jesus Was Remembered*. Salem, OR: Polebridge, 2017.

———. *The Word in Time*. Rev. ed. New Berlin, WI: Liturgical Publications, 1990.

Flannery, Austin, OP, ed. *Vatican Council II: The Basic Sixteen Documents*. Northport, NY: Costello, 1996.

Ford, J. Massyngbaerde. *Redeemer: Friend and Mother*. Minneapolis: Fortress Press, 1997.

Funk, Robert W., Arthur J. Dewey, and the Jesus Seminar. *The Gospel of Jesus*. 2nd ed. Salem, OR: Polebridge, 2015.

Gutiérrez, Gustavo. *On Job*. Maryknoll, NY: Orbis, 1987.

Harrington, Daniel, SJ. *Why Do We Suffer?* Franklin, MO: Sheed & Ward, 2000.

Hauerwas, Stanley. *Naming the Silences*. Grand Rapids: Eerdmans, 1990.

John Paul II. *Catechism of the Catholic Church*. Liguori, MO: Liguori, 1994.

Johnson, Elizabeth. *Quest for the Living God*. New York: Continuum, 2007.

LaCugna, Catherine Mowry. *God for Us*. New York: HarperSanFrancisco, 1991.

MacDonald, Margaret. *Colossians and Ephesians*. Collegeville, MN: Liturgical Press, 2000.

McManus, Kathleen, OP. "Suffering in the Theology of Edward Schillebeeckx." *Theological Studies* 60 (1999): 476–91.

Moloney, Francis. *The Gospel of John*. Collegeville, MN: Liturgical Press, 1998.

Mooney, Christopher, SJ. *Teilhard de Chardin and the Mystery of Christ*. New York: Harper & Row, 1966.

O'Connor, Cardinal John. "Who Will Care for the AIDS Victims?" *Origins* 19, no. 33 (January 18, 1990): 544–48.

O'Donovan, Leo, SJ, ed. *A World of Grace*. Washington, DC: Georgetown University Press, 1995.

Rahner, Karl, SJ. *The Practice of Faith*. New York: Crossroad, 1986.

———. *Theological Investigations IV*. Baltimore: Helicon, 1966.

———. *Theological Investigations V*. Baltimore: Helicon, 1966.

———. *Theological Investigations XI*. New York: Seabury, 1974.

———. *Theological Investigations XIX*. New York: Crossroad, 1983.

Richard, Lucien, OMI. *What Are They Saying about the Theology of Suffering?* Mahwah, NJ: Paulist, 1992.

Romero, Oscar. *The Violence of Love*. San Francisco: Harper & Row, 1988.

Schillebeeckx, Edward. *Christ*. New York: Seabury, 1980.

———. *Jesus*. New York: Seabury, 1979.

Sobrino, Jon. *Where Is God?* Maryknoll, NY: Orbis, 2004.

Tambasco, Anthony. *A Theology of Atonement and Paul's Vision of Christianity*. Collegeville, MN: Liturgical Press, 1991.

Teilhard de Chardin, Pierre, SJ. *How I Believe*. New York: Harper & Row, 1969.

Wink, Walter. *Engaging the Powers*. Minneapolis: Fortress Press, 1992.

———. *The Powers That Be*. New York: Doubleday, 1998.

Winter, Michael. *The Atonement*. Collegeville, MN: Liturgical Press, 1995.

Author Index

Subject Index

Abba, 25–26, 34–35, 71, 74, 91
abyss, 5, 92–94
atonement, 11, 15, 18, 42–43,
    46, 48–49, 54–56, 85
Atonement, Day of, 42, 44

Beatitudes, 79
blood, symbolic significance of,
    42–44, 50, 58
Bread for the World, 82

Colossians, 54, 57–58, 60
compassion, 80–81, 83
consumerism, 6, 83
Corinthians, Letter to, 63
creation for incarnation, 54–67

Daniel, 40–41
Deuteronomy, 13–14, 16, 35, 45
disasters, natural, 12, 16, 85

Ecclesiastes, 17
Ephesians, 54, 57–58, 60–61, 63
Eucharist, 11, 79–80, 90
evolution, 60–62, 66

Francis of Assisi, 60

Galatians, 42
God, goodness of, 25–29;
    images of, 89–94; and the
    incarnation, 53–65; as
    mystery, 58–59, 92–94;
    relationship with Jesus,
    25–26; and suffering of
    Jesus, 17–20
Gospels, writing of, 21–23,
    29–34

Hebrews, 19, 44
Hosea, 91
"How Great Thou Art," 11